P....... -. ..-

Finding Peace with God, Others, and Within

Written & Edited By
Atwannia L. McQueen

Associate Editor & Contributor
J. Tyler

Associate Editor
Taylor Lenore

shirohatoBooks

Published by **shirohatoBooks** ♡

Copyright © 2023 Atwannia L. McQueen

Cover Design, Imprint, & Logo: Taylor Lenore
Author Photo: Robyn Mitch

ISBN 9798329295498
PRINTED IN THE UNITED STATES OF AMERICA

Dear Reader,

*I dedicate this book to **you** and pray you will acknowledge and accept that God's plan will always prevail. God is always at work, and His work has always been and always will be good.*
May you find and know peace with Him, others, and within.

Contents

Preface

This book is a devotional and testimony. It contains scriptural references and prayers relevant to my experiences, as well as actual accounts of my life while transitioning from career wife and mom to nontraditional graduate student and "boomerang child."

There are brief descriptions of circumstances and subsequent emotions and occurrences during this sudden life change and what it entailed. The purpose of this devotional and testimony is to help God's people, who are struggling amid hurt and disappointment, find peace in their lives from the one true source: God. This is not an attempt to pass judgment or exploit the nature of my life nor the people involved in my life in the past or present.

I think it's important to mention that, at the time of publication, my family is learning and practicing extending God's grace and mercy. We are making strides on our respective journeys to understand what it truly means to walk in forgiveness and embrace the peace of the *peaces* (peace with God, each other, and within).

Acknowledgments

God, thank you for being God and loving me. Thank you for being unchanging and gifting me your presence, grace, and mercy through all of life's blessings, joys, hurts, and disappointments. I am grateful for your forgiveness, faithfulness, and protection. I remain in awe of your love, compassion, and peace. I love you.

Tyler, God knew I would need unfiltered honesty, gentleness, patience, determination, and a fighter's spirit and mentality. He blessed you with all those qualities so you could teach me and do so fearlessly. You will always be a sincere joy to me, with your infectious smile and laughter and, most importantly, your uplifting prayers, wisdom, and forgiving, caring heart. The gratitude I feel for the imperfectly perfect son, brother, and teacher you are, fills and nourishes my heart. I praise God for you and the love I discovered when I first saw you. Continue to place all hope and expectation in God. I love you.

Taylor, you are the sweetest overflow of joy. I am honored that you like to say that you are "Tonya 2.0," but sweetheart, I know that I am not even in your league. Your gifts astound me, and your ability to lovingly communicate your heart, with kindness and gentleness of speech and tone, is an inspiration and wisdom that exceeds your years and nothing short of the truth and hand of God on you. I thank God for you and all that He has placed in you that's helped me experience more of Him. You're a beauty beyond physical sight and human understanding. Continue to embrace the gifts of God and the "difference." I love you.

Mom (Lenora), thank you for always kicking me out of every nest you knew I'd settle into and limit myself. I know it cannot have been easy when it's instinctive to pull your child closer and nurture. I am grateful for your direct words—even when I didn't want to hear them. You've taught me to trust and revere God in my most beautiful, hurtful, and vulnerable moments. I understand and appreciate your sacrifices, and I pray that God continues to bless you with peace, joy, and wellness because of your faithfulness. I love you.

Introduction

Bearing Hurt, Seeking Peace

Peace I leave with you, My peace I give to you; not as the world gives do I give to you. Let not your heart be troubled, neither let it be afraid. John 14:27 (NKJV)

They don't want to hear—
Don't want to see—
What this pain is doing to me.
If neither heard nor seen,
Then it is not so—
And they can say,
"We didn't know."

Everyone understood my anger. However, my sadness and disappointment somehow suggested, in their minds, that I preferred a life feeling and being heartsick and broken. As days passed, it became increasingly frustrating to perceive that, even though my life had taken an actual hit and genuine turn, my only tolerable and agreeable emotions had to be counterfeit.

I decided not to speak. The losses kept coming and, the more I lost, the less I spoke. It was so hard to

9

appease expectations. I wanted to feel—I needed to feel, but I couldn't—not really—not what I felt. So, in silence, I carried her. Doctors and specialists advised me that termination was my only option, warning she would only compromise my health. Against their orders, I carried her and, in silence and fear, allowed Hurt to be born. I sometimes called her Grief.

Nursing her made the days weary and tiresome and the nights long and sleepless. She was ravenous. In two months, she weighed fifteen pounds. The doctors and specialists now said Hurt was causing pain in my back, hips, knees, and was the source of my migraines. They said she was too heavy and intense, gave suggestions on how to quiet her, and warned me to stop carrying her around. They said I would feel better if I gave her up.

I couldn't do it. I had earned her. Therefore, I was keeping her. She was mine.

Wary of one more thing that would add insult to my injury and prove itself equally insulting and injurious, in, marched the odds! I was frequently at odds, and odds were consistently against me. Yet, oddly enough, I enrolled in a marriage and family therapy master's program to learn how to be to others what my family and I had needed. My coursework was demanding. Assignments were challenging, causing stifled emotions and buried memories to surface and resurface. I was lonesome, tired, and began noticing that I just did not have the time Hurt required anymore.

Although I neglected her, I was afraid of losing her. I was just so tired. I was tired from not sleeping, but mostly I was tired from crying and living sick…

about who remained silent;

over who would not be quiet;

about who didn't call that said they would;

over who did not answer my call;

about who turned away;

over who I turned away;

about who disregarded and disrespected me;

over who wanted the best for me but gave me their worst;

about feeling and being used;

over being underestimated;

about who didn't show up or when I could not show up;

over who only showed up, for show, expecting a show;

about who didn't have time;

over who refused to make time;

about who misjudged or refused to see Hurt in me;

over brokenness that conceived the brokenness that miscarried and broke me…

About…

Over…

About…

Over…

I was about over it all! What frustrated me most was

how easily I ignored the one who wanted to take the weight of Hurt and carry her so I would not have to; the one who wanted to wean me of her…

God,
The broken pieces of me need peace to see—
Everything you're doing in me.
If hurt, shame and brokenness are parts of your plan,
Then calm, shade, and uphold me with thy hand.
The storms keep coming.
Only you can make them cease.
Only you, God, can turn broken pieces into peaces of me.

In asking God for peace, He showed me I needed it in various areas of my life. He changed my perspective so I was able to see that, in Him, I could be free and not at odds or in conflict despite my environment, experiences, or circumstances.

Peaces of Me is a devotional and testimony with scriptures, prayers, and stories of discovering God's goodness on my journey to healing and peace. It is my prayer that you may take away even one scripture, prayer, or story that will give a piece of you the peace of God.

Peace One

The Book Cover

*The God of my rock; in him will I trust: he is my
shield, and the horn of my salvation, my high tower,
and my refuge, my saviour; thou savest me from
violence. 2 Samuel 22:3 (KJV)*

When she was nine years old, I took my daughter to
visit an allergist, and my mom accompanied us. A
nurse remarked that my daughter was so sweet and
looked like she would be that way all the time. My
mom put an arm around my daughter, looked down at
her, and said, "Don't judge a book by its cover! You
have moments like anyone else, right 'Little Girl?'" My
daughter responded, "That's right!" My mom gave her
a squeeze as they laughed.

We say, "Don't judge a book by its cover," to
discourage assumptions made about ourselves, other
people, or things based on how they may physically
appear. What if we considered and used that phrase
spiritually and metaphorically to recognize what God
perceives in us and how He cares for and protects us?

If, figuratively, we are books, then our physical
appearance is the covering of our pages bound together

by life experiences (both good and bad), and Jesus is the book cover. A book cover surrounds the actual cover or skin of a book to protect it, keep it safe, and guard it from damage resulting from use. Scripture tells us that God is our shield, our rescuer, and protector. God keeps us from becoming worn and torn by life. Therefore, what another person sees is not always an accurate preview of our untold stories, our desperation in distress, or longings that stem from disappointment and rejection, which are often reasons we seek God's protection. He safeguards and preserves us, and we are covered securely by the fortress of His love and grace.

Personally, there are times I know my physical appearance is confusing or misleading. There is pain I may never share; therefore, I permit others to see only what I want, and as much as I want, of what remains untold. The one thing I have felt most in control of is what I allow my physical cover to show, which I usually determine from the freedom I feel in my environments. Yet, I know that in my life's most tumultuous times, it is the spiritual covering of God that surpasses what I willingly reveal. That remains true as I strive to find peace and heal while learning more about God, His Word, and what it means to lean on and trust Him with every care.

The depth of the shame of failure, at the loss of love and family the way I wanted it to be, is not what you'll see when I'm strolling grocery store aisles. I used to worry that smiling, feeling genuine cheer, or allowing myself to experience laughter while suffering, made me appear ignorant of my circumstances and insincere. However, I have come to understand that to know God means knowing I can experience His joy even when I'm in pain. His promise to turn sorrow into joy is not a spontaneous occurrence once the dust settles and smoke clears from life's battles. Joy is readily available in the solace of His Word, in prayer with Him, and in slowing down to trust and obey. Therefore, when I smile, despite what I am going through, it is neither deceptive, conflicting, nor a contradiction, since I know the one who shields, covers, and protects me!

We are books covered by the best covering we could ask for or have. Whether our experiences and physical appearances show and tell sadness and defeat or happiness and strength, there is peace to be known and experienced in the sovereign book cover who keeps us set apart, hedged, upheld, favored, and shaded!

Lord, grant me peace with how I see myself. Help me to see as you, my covering, covers me. Amen.

Faith-Walking

The Lord God is my strength; He will make my feet like deer's feet, And He will make me walk on my high hills. Habakkuk 3:19 (NKJV)

There was a season of my life I felt like I was completely drowning under problem after situation after issue. I was upset all the time and worried about the unfairness of suffering for things that were not my fault. In fact, that worry is what became my focus—my obsession even. I simply could not make sense of my predicament. I confided in a lady from church and was prepared for scriptures, prayers, and validation. Instead, I became engaged in an unwanted discussion about accountability. I couldn't hear her, nor did I want to! There was no way I was going to be blamed for the current state of affairs disguised as my life!

My family, my life—nothing was as I had known or hoped for, and I needed answers—not a mirror. Like Habakkuk, I questioned and desired reasons why God would allow this to happen—why He would allow my heart to be in so much pain. There were moments in prayer that I would angrily cry, "God, you knew this was coming, and you didn't bother to tell me—knowing what it would do to me"! I worried and wondered when things would let up and if I would ever recover.

Scripture reminds us that we must come to terms with life's high hills and sufferings. I now understand the point that the lady from church was making. Accountability, in my case, was not about an admission of fault, rather it was a nudge to accept my life's current terms and rely on God and his strength instead of scolding Him.

It is important to lament—to share our pain, anger, and disappointment when we are communicating with God. However, in doing so, we must also willingly align ourselves in submission to God's will and ways; profess our hope in Him and His Word; and faith-walk. Faith-walking is allowing the mind and sight of God to guide us where we need to be, while we are in or moving through and beyond where circumstances insist that we are stuck and end.

Having feet like a deer, as the scripture describes, means being able to maneuver above what life and this world make us believe is allowed or even possible. It is also a figurative description for how God's strength helps us to glide gently, stand firm, yet remain soft in life's rough places and hard moments. Our faith-walk is not blind; we have His plan and revelation. It is not mindless; we have His assured presence and power. Regardless of what is visible or perceived ahead, we walk in the ways God has called us and into what He wills. His strength keeps us from destruction under the weight of any oppression.

Life may not feel great right now. There may be things happening that are not on the terms you desired or imagined. Do not surrender your faith. Resist scolding God. Make and hold yourself accountable to relying on him, his love, and protection.

Thank you, God, for the strength to trust and believe in you. I only want to see what you see in the ways that you see. Guide me so I might be at peace on my faith-walk. You are my help and hope. Amen.

His Children, His Punishment, His Timing

There will be trouble and distress for every human being who does evil: first for the Jew, then for the Gentile... For God does not show favoritism.
Romans 2:9,11 (NIV)

People, often those closest to us, can hurt us in ways sometimes that feel and sound unimaginable unless witnessed or experienced. It can feel like God made a grand exit at just the moments we need Him most.

There have been times I found myself crying and screaming at God, "Are you seriously not seeing this?" I was incredibly distressed, knowing I had become the object of others' pain and hurt. While I remained a stagnated and utterly emotional wreck and heartbroken, they appeared to move on. God was not punishing them...as far as I could see.

From my perspective, moving on seemed like a foreign concept. How could I move on unless God did something about the injustices I had suffered and my offenders? When I would express how I felt to a friend, she would encourage me to simply pray.

I laugh now when I think of how I told her that I would read her messages and mumble in frustration, "If she says 'pray' one more time…!" Still, she remained firm in asking me to pray that God guard my heart and give me wisdom and direction.

I was over it all—her prayer suggestions—her meekness… I wanted justice and, if I was going to do all this praying she suggested, I wanted to pray that God rain down fire on every source of my kids' and my hurt and inconveniences!

As I am still journeying to peace, I am most grateful she would not let up on prayer. There were mornings I would awaken to a simple message from her: "I'm still praying for you."

Hurt can cause us to become so caught up in what is not happening to our perpetrators that we forget God's role and our own role in our lives. According to scripture, God is the deliverer of justice, *not us*, and He is not selective when it comes to injustices. He does not show favoritism, nor does He overlook or leave sins and malicious acts toward another unpunished.

I confess it seemed more important to ponder when God was going to do something about the people who hurt me than to pray and be in relationship with Him. Justice was what I needed and felt I deserved. It would prove He heard me and cared. I felt confident that it would also clear up any misconceptions about me and confirm that I was not the problem. It troubled me how my desired justice did not appear to be as swift and was not as conspicuous as the hurt I experienced.

Submitting to God's authority can be hard when we want so desperately for the hurt to stop and to feel a sense of vindication and retribution. However, proving ourselves or disproving what anyone believes or misconceives should not be our focus or responsibility. Neither should the witnessing nor overseeing of justice be our chief concern. There must be a greater urgency to learn and commit to accepting that those who hurt us are God's children, and He will always deal with them in His way and in His time. We must surrender daily to the will of God and find peace in His timing.

Lord, I need peace while learning to accept and respect your timing and the mercy and compassion you have for each of us. Forgive those who have hurt me; forgive me; and help me find peace in doing the same. Amen.

Peace Four

Breaking-Silence

Rescue those being led away to death; hold back those staggering toward slaughter. If you say, "But we knew nothing about this," does not he who weighs the heart perceive it? Does not he who guards your life know it? Will he not repay everyone according to what they have done? Proverbs 24:11-12 (NIV)

Have you ever said or heard someone else say, "it's not my place," to justify not wanting to intervene on someone's behalf? Do you convince yourself that it is not your responsibility to become involved in or vocal about grievances that aren't directly applicable to you, because doing so won't make a real difference or matter? When you've heard an unedifying conversation or witnessed an unjust act, did you predict you would receive a negative reaction, and choose to remain silent?

There are times when the loudest and boldest demonstrations of people who do not care can prove to be no match for the resounding, deafening silence of people who say that they do. Our greatest hurts can intensify and deepen after we share our hearts with family and friends and experience and learn their silence. During those most unstable years and seasons of watching my family fall apart, no word ever spoken could have prepared me for all the silence. Silence broke me in ways that, without God, I didn't think I would ever feel whole again.

Our silence can be physical as well as spiritual. When we ignore words spoken against another that cause dissension, strife, and harm, or disregard the increasing severity of another's plight, God will examine our motives and circumstances. The scripture reference reminds us of our responsibility to serve others by helping them and protecting their lives when they're in need. While it may not always be possible or necessary to posture ourselves to physically approach and assist someone, God has taught us to pray according to *Matthew* 6:13, "deliver **us** from evil…". Whether we are hurting or caring for someone who is hurting, collectively we need God's peace and comfort. We can support and help each other by covering one another in prayer. God will provide us and those around us with the words to pray appropriately and strengthen us to speak to one another in ways that make our messages receptive.

My grandmother used to say that even if we didn't exactly do anything wrong, lingering around or remaining in the presence of wrongdoing would make us open to blame and punishment. The same is true of our silence. The enemy desires to spiritually slaughter God's people so that we feel defeated and distance ourselves from Him. When Christians make excuses to keep quiet or say, "it's not my place," we do not avoid accountability. Instead, we position ourselves to become complicit in allowing evil to access our brothers and sisters in Christ.

Dear Lord, when I see others in situations that may harm them or their relationship with you, teach me how to respond. When I cannot speak to my loved one or friend, give me the willingness to speak to you on his or her behalf. Help me to find no peace in silence that leaves your people broken. Enable me to help keep your people alive spiritually with my prayers and support. Amen.

Peace Five

Energy

Therefore be imitators of God as dear children. And walk in love, as Christ also has loved us and given Himself for us, ... Ephesians 5:1-2 (NKJV)

I was speaking over the phone with a childhood friend, and the subject of "matching energy" in relationships came up. I expressed that I simply can't do it because it means I'm not being myself or allowing the other person to be who he or she is. The idea of being or becoming what causes me discomfort or hurts me, so I can feel I have an advantage, feels like I am surely giving that advantage away!

Scripture tells us that we are to follow and act like Christ—not like people. When we walk in love, we carry within us the spirit of Christ, who is gracious, merciful, and unchanging.

Social media or catch phrases and cliches in social settings make it sound like matching the energy in the room is appropriate or protects your peace and sense of self. However, we should not be this easily influenced by others' behaviors nor feel an inclination to compliment and imitate them and define that as protection. We may not be able to elect and control the actions of others, but we are able to determine our own. We need to decide that no matter what is staring back at us, we will only reflect God—His image, truth, heart, and nature.

Inside each of us, are experiences that have created feelings or issues remaining well after the experiences occurred. As a result, we have developed mismatched words and facial expressions in our attempts to cope with the effects of trauma, loss, disappointment, or abandonment. Bad or unwanted energy, when nursed and nurtured by mirroring and matching, only prepares ground for growing contempt and confusion, which are not of God. When we try to match someone's energy, we are often matching his or her responses to hurts that we could quite possibly help and/or heal by matching and imitating God and His character instead.

My current journey, and it is ongoing, demands that I find peace in respecting another's disposition while continuing to respect and maintain my own. Matching or imitating peoples' ever-changing and unpredictable energies distracts me from who God desires me to be and how He has instructed and demonstrated I should behave.

Lord, when I am tempted to match and save face, yield me your peace to act in love and extend grace. Amen.

Peace Six

Don't Confuse Pleasure with Treasure

*Lay not up for yourselves treasures upon earth, where
moth and rust doth corrupt, and where thieves break
through and steal: But lay up for yourselves treasures
in heaven, where neither moth nor rust doth corrupt,
and where thieves do not break through nor steal: For
where your treasure is, there will your heart be also.*
Matthew 6:19-21 (KJV)

On a trip to the grocery store with my son, who at
that time was six years old, I was standing at a freezer
and staring indecisively at pints of butter pecan and
rum raisin ice-cream. He asked, "Mom, if it makes your
stomach hurt, why do you eat it"? I laughed and said,
"I just really love ice-cream!" He responded, "In music,
we sing, 'Where Your Treasure Is, There Your Heart
Will Be'!" He proceeded to sing with all his might right
there on the frozen foods aisle!

An insatiable thirst for family, connection, and
relationship has been the source of choices and/or
behaviors that have left me questioning who I am. The
highs of fulfilling whimsical moments with people and
indulgences always crashed in lows that left me

repeatedly in want. It just didn't make sense that God could be my *every*, *single*, *thing*. What did He have to do with my love of ice-cream? He can't be ice-cream! He can't be what I long for in my relationships!

When I reflect on being my heaviest at 202 pounds and pre-diabetic, ice-cream had filled the voids of lonely nights and stifled my voice which wasn't desired to be heard. I had not fully comprehended God's desire to hear me, nor that He would speak to me and let me know He loved me and cared. It never occurred to me that God and I could truly spend time together and, although He was not physically present, I could physically feel His presence. Food and people were pleasures that I made treasures and, when they made me feel poorly, I self-medicated by consuming more food and begging for the presence of people who repeatedly showed me they were not either emotionally or otherwise available.

The treasures of God are His Word and works that He so graciously gives to us. His promises of love and relationship are for us to possess for eternity. The pleasures we pursue are opposites—only providing temporary comfort and having momentary value or importance. Whether it's money, careers, material possessions—even food and people—we tend to gratify ourselves or satisfy our needs and habits with what is often self- compromising, self-destructive, and perishable at the hands of others in pursuit of the very same things.

Scripture advises us not to make worldly pleasures our treasures and displace our focus, values, priorities, or time. We must not become preoccupied with making the world's temptations and rewards or our faulty default behaviors substitutions for the comfort and satisfaction only God can provide.

It has been vital for me, on my peace and healing journey, to stop prioritizing ice-cream-like pleasures that are self-detrimental and start clinging to God and His lasting treasures. It's become most important that **He** has my heart.

What pleasures are you making your treasures? Consider then, who or what has your heart.

Lord, I need peace in my heart and mind. Help me take pleasure in making you my treasure today and every day. Amen.

Peace Seven

Unfaithful

Ye adulterers and adulteresses, know ye not that the friendship of the world is enmity with God? whosoever therefore will be a friend of the world is the enemy of God. James 4:4 (KJV)

During a mid-week grocery-run, after she had asked multiple probing questions consecutively regarding my responses to recent stressors, I confessed to my mother that, at age 48, I struggle with both belonging and fitting in. While I would like to be myself, I don't necessarily feel I'm enough or that I'm completely safe to do so. I am also unable to fully commit to being someone I'm not in order to feel accepted.

There are those people who fear missing out and those who fear not measuring up or feel discontent with how they are faring in contrast to their peers socially, professionally, and financially. Well, after being a housewife and homeschool mom; not working outside of the home for almost 19 years; and being forced into a position of starting over after being in a relationship and marriage with my husband for over half my life; it would be accurate to say I have fears, insecurities, and discontent in *every* area!

When I was ready to admit to loved ones that my marriage was over, I attended events at their suggestions and assertions that I deserved some time out and should be enjoying myself. They meant well, and I was desperate to fit in but ashamed to admit that I was grieving. To assist me with getting reestablished, a few of them offered or suggested various employment opportunities. I applied for jobs because I wanted them to feel I desired more, even though I knew I was just grief-struck and stuck. I couldn't think of work, especially when, in my heart, I did not think a particular job was one God intended. I was not going to waste any more of my life and time where I wasn't wanted nor desired to be. Yet, feeling I needed their approval and acceptance, I applied but expressed false disappointment when my efforts were unsuccessful.

Family and friends, with the best intentions, will often advise us on where we should be, what we should know and do, and how we should show up in the world amid trials or in response to our circumstances. The Word tells us in *Exodus* 34:14 that God is jealous, and we are to only worship and focus on Him and what He wills and desires. The scripture reference from *James* raises the level of emphasis by comparing succumbing to the world's desires for our lives to committing adultery or being unfaithful to God. Sadly, I must admit it was the depth of my need to feel accepted, especially during this season of loss, loneliness, and foreign responsibilities and beginnings, which conceived my own unfaithfulness. I am yet learning, however, that it is impossible to have faith in what God wills and desires for me and still meet everyone's expectations and require their affirmation.

I once viewed a social media post about being comfortable with not having a life update that either fits or helps one fit into social/societal norms and expectations. The post stressed that we can be content with being in a position of simply waiting on God, and *waiting* is a comfort space and sufficient life update.

Do you find yourself condoning or conforming to beliefs and behaviors to fit into your relationship with the world? Do you alter or dismiss what you know God has called you to, so that you can keep up with others or where the world says you should be? The scripture expresses the seriousness of commitment in relationship with God. It communicates the enormity and significance of making peace with trusting in Him as our God and leader; having peace in following Him only; and being at peace with remaining faithful to His wisdom and plans concerning who we should be, where we should be, and His ability to establish us there.

Dear Lord, forgive me for compromising our relationship. Help me in my efforts to be faithful to you. I desire peace in your plans for me and to become someone you can trust with them. Amen.

Peace Eight

Remember Who You're Talking To

He who has knowledge spares his words, And a man of understanding is of a calm spirit.
Proverbs 17:27 (NKJV)

My son has always been a gentle soul and, for me, a most influential teacher. Watching him over the years with his sister has been the best parenting course. He has helped me become more self-aware and create a safe space for constructive communication.

I was speaking to my daughter candidly one morning and asked her to name something she would like me to work on or an area in which she felt I could be better as a mom. She replied, "I would just say…work on not snapping and remember who you're talking to." I couldn't help but chuckle at her honesty— after all, I did ask!

Life had sucker-punched me very hard, and I was nowhere I desired to be—in any capacity. I struggled daily with the joint decision to become a homemaker that left me financially unequipped to independently give my children the home and life for which they were set up. Nothing, in which they had collectively been

given hope and comfort, was being authored. I was furious with myself for my part in it all, and it was showing.

On morning walks or at night when no one else was awake, I would ask God to please make this situation right as though it was never wrong and give us back what we lost. My frustration and sheer annoyance with our new unfamiliar order and routines were planting a bitterness that made my eyes scolding and my tongue biting at innocent sweetness and love, while also diminishing hope in what God could do for us through me.

I agreed with my daughter, and I was proud of her ability and courage to express herself. I needed to be mindful of my tone, who I am talking to, and what comes out in pain.

The scripture affirms that knowledge and understanding are both meaningful for communication that is controlled and gracious. In relationship with God, there is access to the knowledge He imparts; therefore, we know what He desires for us to do. We also receive an understanding that the Holy Spirit teaches us to comprehend why we should obey. God loves us; He is mindful of, merciful, generous, and gentle with us. Knowledge advises and understanding reveals that we should be the same when speaking to one another and ourselves because they, and we, are children of God!

The enemy can be tricky and cause us to react to life's challenges and exchanges with people according to our perception or interpretation of consequential feelings and emotions we have brewing inside. My daughter was saying, "I am not who or what's eating at you! I'm your baby! Remember who you're talking to!" As Christians, we must learn to seek God and make peace with what is happening to us, as well as inside of us, so we may be mindful of what comes out. We need to use our words godly, wisely, and pay attention and remember to whom and whose we are speaking!

Lord, thank you for reminding me to speak as you would speak. Forgive me for my missteps as I grow in faith, peaceful communication, and in remembering who and whose we all are in Christ. Amen.

Keep it Real...Quiet

Now a leper came to Him, imploring Him, kneeling down to Him and saying to Him, "If You are willing, You can make me clean." Then Jesus, moved with compassion, stretched out His hand and touched him, and said to him, "I am willing; be cleansed." As soon as He had spoken, immediately the leprosy left him, and he was cleansed. And He strictly warned him and sent him away at once, and said to him, "See that you say nothing to anyone; but go your way, show yourself to the priest, and offer for your cleansing those things which Moses commanded, as a testimony to them." However, he went out and began to proclaim it freely, and to spread the matter, so that Jesus could no longer openly enter the city, but was outside in deserted places; and they came to Him from every direction. Mark 1:40-41, 43-45 (NKJV)

It has become a common and frequent practice today to share intimate details of your life via media platforms. In fact, the more information you're willing to disclose and the more remarkable that information is perceived, then the more you are recognized for "keeping it real," "keeping it one hundred," and celebrated for being an authentic and/or "real" person.

We are often subjected to challenges in life where we encounter instances of internal and external encouragement, pressure, and temptation to tell our experiences to anyone who will listen; but, to what end? Are we trying to bring others to Christ, offer them hope, and tell them about the one and only true survival option that is Jesus?

In retrospect, it seems surreal that anyone would suggest that I discuss my marriage and family over social media outlets at a time when hurts and wounds were fresh, and feelings and emotions were running most high and volatile. Concerned this might be a poor decision—as it was completely out of character for me and seemed counterproductive to my simply feeling better or making it through a day without tears, I asked my mom to share her thoughts. She said, "When it's time for you to talk, you will know, and you won't have to ask what anyone else or I think. You'll be at peace about it."

When I did start to find a sense of peace about how to best manage and respond to my marital and familial conditions, God did not lead me to media platforms but instead prompted me to pursue my master's in marriage and family therapy. I shared with one of my professors on exercising the skill of self-disclosure in future practice that, in professional instances, where it might prove helpful, I would feel comfortable and find it appropriate to reference my subjective experiences. It is my prayer that they might encourage individuals and couples to feel hopeful, to hope in God, and find and embrace help and healing.

Respectfully, there are people God instructs to speak candidly and in-depth about their lives on platforms which, in salient ways, help others. However, there are also persons, like the man with leprosy, whom Jesus has asked to say nothing. When we are instructed to be silent about our stories, it is to serve **Him**, *His* purpose, *His* will, and *His* timely reveal.

The leper mishandled an opportunity for partnership with Jesus. He desired the leper's discretion so that He could continue to preach and teach. However, the leper's disobedience shifted the focus from Jesus' Word to His works, proving that sometimes the details derail.

Every aspect of our stories is not intended to be shared, nor are certain details to be shared with every individual. Some information does not support the move of God; but instead, serves as a distraction or creates opportunities for chatter and idle conversations. Sometimes keeping it real means keeping quiet and staying true to God's purpose for your life and story.

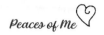

Decide that you will accept and remain in partnership with Him. Ask what He wills you to say, as well as to whom you should say it, and for peace in awaiting His perfectly timed disclosure.

Lord, thank you for entrusting my life, its experiences, and challenges to me. Thank you for peace in quietness that keeps us connected while you move in the lives of your people. Amen.

Peace Ten

That's the Joy

Consider it pure joy, my brothers and sisters, whenever you face trials of many kinds, because you know that the testing of your faith produces perseverance. James 1:2-3 (NIV)

It was a rainy Monday morning I sat in the car thinking, "*Really* God?" My ophthalmologist's words, "optic nerve damage" and "glaucoma" kept ringing in my ears and echoing in my head. Every appointment in that office, from that day on, was pure torture. I simply resented the fact that I had to be there! My marriage was crumbling, and here I was again, dealing with yet another health issue that stress had either catalyzed or could exacerbate. I was sick of being sick. I was also sick of hearing that word: **stress**. What sickened me most was that every diagnosis preceded a walk to the car and drive to where I knew empathy, love, and genuine care had residence but did not live where I wanted and needed them most.

Months following my glaucoma diagnosis, I was visiting my then hair stylist and venting about my diagnosis and subsequent appointments being spiritually and emotionally depleting and defeating. My ophthalmologist had, by now, prescribed two different eye-drops; but both were ineffective; and I had suffered more nerve damage. Now that I write those words and, as I read them, I can't believe I told her that what I found *most* disheartening about it all was, the only people in the lobby my age accompanied elderly patients who always seemed to be staring at me. Her response was, "Girl, those elderly people are probably looking at you and saying, 'God is a keeper! Look at her! We could've been in here a lot sooner'!" I burst into laughter in spite of myself!

The scripture reference from *James* reminds us to change how we look at our trials. We should see them as joy: things that come to make our faith stronger so that we become long-suffering, patient, learn to place our hope in God, and acquire peace we cannot begin to comprehend. He is not saying we need to feel happy about loss, illness, or any suffering. We should, however, see them as experiences that deeply root and secure our trust in the knowledge and belief that, by His Word and presence, God will support and guide us through life's changes and challenges. That's the joy!

If I take what the stylist said and try to see the joy in that experience, then I can look in the faces of those elderly patients and agree that God is indeed a keeper, and He will keep me too!

My Father in Heaven, thank you for trials that plant a deeper trust in you and offer peace in believing and rejoicing. Amen.

Good God, Good Grief

*Praise be to the God and Father of our Lord Jesus
Christ, the Father of compassion and the God of all
comfort, who comforts us in all our troubles, so that
we can comfort those in any trouble with the comfort
we ourselves receive from God.*
2 Corinthians 1:3-4 (NIV)

"Good grief;" what a contradiction! Seriously, what could be good about grief? Although grief may be felt at the loss of possessions, it is often felt in response to the loss of people: the death of someone or the end of a relationship. Extremely volatile and stressful environments, trials, and troubles can also cause grievous feelings and emotions. The phrase, "Good grief!" is sometimes used to express frustration and as a substitution for the exclamative clause, "Good god!"

When we consider the words themselves and the scripture, what if Christians used them as an affirmation of who God is in our time of grieving? What if we used them to proclaim God's comfort and its purpose?

The goodness of grief is the comfort of the Lord. If we were to take the time and consider for a moment the often physical and mental afflictions of grief: *the depths of emotions and feelings that take root in our minds and bodies in the aftermath of hurt and disappointment—as we are yet surviving, healing, and experiencing His peace*—then we would see the goodness of God and how abundant his comfort is! Even whispering to yourself, "Good God—" not as a casual exclamative, rather as a proclamation and declaration—becomes, for us, an affirming reminder that our God is good! He is so good that He will give an overflow of comfort that we can in turn offer His people.

In our grief, God is teaching us; He is sustaining us; He is making us user-friendly; and He's making it work for good—like He said He would. The scripture assures us of God's presence in grief, so use the phrase to feel it and allow yourself to be present with Him.

Say: I'm sad, but good God, good grief! I am hurting, but good God, good grief! I'm lonely now, but good God, good grief! Fill in the words that best suit your circumstances, knowing that, despite what you are going through, God's comfort is abounding and available, and He does not stop being good!

Lord, you save me daily! Thank you for your comfort.

Thank you for the peace that floods me with the assurance that, even in grief, you are a good God! Amen.

Who is He to You?

*Now He could do no mighty work there, except that
He laid His hands on a few sick people and healed
them. And He marveled because of their unbelief.
Then He went about the villages in a circuit, teaching.
Mark 6:5-6 (NKJV)*

*So all those in the synagogue, when they heard these
things, were filled with wrath, and rose up and thrust
Him out of the city; and they led Him to the brow of
the hill on which their city was built, that they might
throw Him down over the cliff. Luke 4:28-29 (NKJV)*

*He said to them, "But who do you say that I am?"
Peter answered and said, "The Christ of God."
Luke 9:20 (NKJV)*

Jesus encountered people who essentially wanted to
have their cake and eat it too. They were doubtful and
did not acknowledge Him as the Son of God, but they
wanted to experience His healing miracles.

According to the scripture reference, when the
disciples shared the names crowds of people were
calling Him, Jesus then questioned the disciples about
who *they* say He is. Peter's answer told Him what He

already knew: Peter had not allowed people to influence him and cause him to become conflicted or doubt who Jesus is.

There are times when what we hear or experience changes our image of God, especially when we compare our encounters with negative exchanges and interactions to the God we know and/or desire to know. It saddens me to admit that repetitive love-hurts created a cynicism that shifted my perspective of God, expectations in Him, and relationship with Him. I felt if He would allow such huge, hurtful, life-altering experiences, it was because He must have thought little of me, and my life wasn't important. In response, I belittled myself often and, when others did the same, it seemed more like home than dislocation.

I planted my heart deeply in people, places, and spaces where the hurt was most intense. Like the people in the scripture reference, I doubted God while also expecting His miracles. There were times I found myself pitting God against my hardships and never betting in His favor but wanting His favor most desperately. When, despite my prayers and pleas, nothing seemingly changed or there was no apparent blessing from God nor discernable evidence of His redemptive work to report, I'd tell myself that it was par for the course and confirmed His lack of care for me. It was easy to pray and believe for others but difficult to have the same steadfastness in God for myself when troubled. It escaped me that God was being a loving God and saving me by allowing the hurtful rejections; providing for me with the painful revelations; and protecting me with His grace and mercy despite my disobedience. In those moments of my deepest pain, loss, and loneliness, God was opening doors leading me to a life and love He prepared and inviting me into relationship with Him, where I could truly feel and be at home.

If we are not careful, we can allow circumstances and false messages and influences to define our relationship with God and who He is in our lives. Jesus already knew what Peter's answer would be. His question is important because it prompts us to examine our own faithfulness and whether we truly believe God, and in Him, or only respect and expect His works and miracles.

This exchange with Peter is also encouragement for us to remain firm in our belief in who God is—no matter what anyone or anything else suggests. Who is He to you? When circumstances toss you about, is He your refuge and leveler or the object of your blame and anger? Do you allow your circumstances to tell you what to think about God, or do you find rest and peace in His Word and truth?

Circumstances say you are lonely; is He still a

friend, a mother and father who won't leave you nor forsake you, or is He a fair-weather friend and deserter who gave up on you? Who is He to you? When you hear defeating messages that say you can't go on and you won't make it, do you still regard Him as your savior who will strengthen and uphold you, or do you think of Him as a mere saboteur, undermining your efforts and keeping you discouraged? Who is He to you? When experiences and appearances suggest you've got your act together, and you are confident, blessed and favored, is He the Good Shepherd who's worthy of honor and praise, or is He emergency box God, and you only break the glass in a crisis? Who is He to you?

Lord, I only find peace by believing in you and trusting and believing you. Thank you for being who you say you are and doing what you say you will. Amen.

The Cry and Crier

In my distress I called upon the Lord, and cried unto my God: he heard my voice out of his temple, and my cry came before him, even into his ears.
Psalm 18:6 (KJV)

My mom and I joke about our cries. I say that I cry ugly, and she says she looks ugly when she cries. Nevertheless, we cry.

I personally feel like the loudest cries to God are the ones you cry in solitude, or in the presence of others where no sound escapes, and when you cannot utter a single word because you have none that are sufficiently expressive. Only God knows; only He hears what you cannot speak.

We cry under various circumstances: when experiencing joy or sadness; when grieving or in mourning; or when lonely or discouraged. My mom and I joke about what our cries make us look and sound like, but what we are really describing is how crying makes us vulnerable—sometimes to the comprehension and misconceptions of another's eyes and ears. When we cry, certain aspects of ourselves we often repress or would not typically divulge become exposed.

When others see our tears or hear our cries, they may assume that we are hurting or sad, but they do not really know what our tears are saying. I love how the scripture emphasizes that God hears our cries, using the words, "even into His ears." You see, because of who God is, I know it is not just incomprehensible sounds He hears. God hears the actual words being shed!

Our cries and tears pour, from deep places in our hearts, the words we cannot even begin to think to speak, and God hears what they say. So, do not hold back your tears because they are prayers to your Father in Heaven, who hears what anxious discomfort drops say. He comprehends the story that sorrowful sobs tell, and He attends to the wound weeps' whispers about what was done and where it hurts.

Whether you cry ugly, like I do, or look ugly when you cry, like my mom, cry to God; find peace in allowing your cries into His ears!

My Father in Heaven, words escape me. I am at such a loss because the lingering awfulness of hurts and pain permeates deeply. I need you. Lord, only you can hear and comprehend the words of my tears and bring my heart and mind peace. Amen.

Peace Fourteen

A Matter of Heart and Mind

*Set your affection on things above, not on things on
the earth. Colossians 3:2 (KJV)
And be not conformed to this world: but be ye
transformed by the renewing of your mind, that ye
may prove what is that good, and acceptable, and
perfect, will of God. Romans 12:2 (KJV)*

Sometimes, in our relationships, including those
with friends and family, we find ourselves revisiting
the same conversations or issues repeatedly. I felt
strongly that an estranged setting of the heart (a heart
alienated from God) and fickleness of mind created
inconsistencies that were cruel detriments to my
marriage and life. There was so much confusion and
sheer exhaustion from the repetitive resurfacing of the
same issues, disappointments, and disagreements,
making it so that a huge chunk of my life since youth,
came to a steady, deliberate, and inevitable end. This is
what can happen in relationships when individuals lack
the ability to see that the stability of the mind and
firmness of the relationship's foundation are contingent
on the heart being set on God's Word, His truth, and

53

things of His nature and spirit—not the world's expectations or clichés.

The scriptures address both the heart and mind because they both matter. When we set our affections on the things above, we root our hearts in uncompromising, unconditional truth. In a world where everything is constantly changing, that means not being easily accessible to anyone or anything that does not serve God's truth, love, grace, mercy, or the peace that He desires to pour into our lives so that we might pour into the lives of others. When we renew our minds, we do so with the understanding that it changes frequently, based on how we feel, making its commitment to change more challenging and inconsistent. Therefore, it is important where we set our hearts and that we renew our minds to accurately reflect that setting.

Hearts not set on the things of God are hearts distant, out of position, or divorced from His will. They are more vulnerable when tempted or attacked. If your heart is under attack, without the renewing of your mind, you are more likely to entertain conflicting thoughts that distance you from God's positioning and His will. You become susceptible to behaviors that compromise your relationship with God and others.

Lord, I give my heart and the matters of my heart to you. I pray for peace in my relationships. Help me in my efforts to set my heart and renew my mind so that I might focus and have peace and contentment with you. Help me so I do not become easily distracted or swayed by feeling, thinking, or behaving in ways that are not of you and cause my relationships to suffer. Please do the same for those with whom I have relationships. Amen.

Drawn Out of "This"

For I, the Lord your God, will hold your right hand,
Saying to you, 'Fear not, I will help you."
Isaiah 41:13 (NKJV)
But when she could hide him no longer, she got a
papyrus basket for him and coated it with tar and
pitch. Then she placed the child in it and put it among
the reeds along the bank of the Nile. His sister stood
at a distance to see what would happen to him. Then
his sister asked Pharaoh's daughter, "Shall I go and
get one of the Hebrew women to nurse the baby for
you?" "Yes, go," she answered. So the girl went and
got the baby's mother. Pharaoh's daughter said to
her, "Take this baby and nurse him for me, and I will
pay you." So the woman took the baby and nursed
him. When the child grew older, she took him to
Pharaoh's daughter and he became her son. She
named him Moses, saying, "I drew him out of the
water." Exodus 2:3-4, 7-10 (NIV)

Sometimes we are put in situations and places and
have exchanges with people that leave us drowning in
confusion, worry, or hurt, while telling God, "I don't

think I'm going to make it, because it's just too much!"
Then, someone near and dear says, or a media person
posts, "You've got this!" I don't know about you, but I
find myself thinking, "I surely do not have *this*! If I had
this, then I wouldn't be in *this*, and then all *this* would
not be happening!" Even still, I am inclined to believe
we find ourselves in situations and places, and
interacting with certain people that challenge our
comforts, faith, and beliefs, because such instances are
usually when we seek God sincerely, desiring to know
His promises and provisions concerning our lives.

The scripture references provide comfort in
knowing that God will help us. The story of Moses is
further proof of God's love, faithfulness, and the
fulfillment of His promises to prepare our way and
remain. Moses's mother was put in the difficult,
delicate position of having to protect him by placing
him in a basket and water without certainty of his fate,
but God did not forget her. Miriam, her daughter, was
able to watch Moses and be in position to ensure that
he was nursed by their mother. Although Moses was
placed in the basket and water, God did not forsake
him. He did not suffer harm nor did he drown. God had
every "*this*" of each person in that story! We don't have
to be worried, anxious, or afraid. Just as God made
provisions for Moses and his mother, He has made
them for us.

It is okay to feel and know you don't "got this"! However, know that your savior does! Trust, believe, feel, and accept the peace that comes from knowing that God has whatever "this" you've been placed in, and He won't allow you to simply be cast out or forgotten. With His hand on your, "*this*," you can face it! God will help you! He has prepared the way and will draw you out!

*God, you know what **this** is! You know what **this** has done. Thank you for your provisions I did not see and those for which you are preparing me. There are days that feel harder—darker—but my faith remains in you! My hope and expectation are in you! Thank you for the peace that comes from knowing you have not forgotten me, and it is you who will see me through **this** and draw me out of **this**, because **you've got this**! Amen.*

Peace Sixteen

User-Friendly

*Trust in the Lord with all thine heart; and lean not
unto thine own understanding. In all thy ways
acknowledge him, and he shall direct thy paths.
Proverbs 3:5-6 (KJV)
Thou hast commanded us to keep thy precepts
diligently. O that my ways were directed to keep thy
statutes! Then shall I not be ashamed, when I have
respect unto all thy commandments.
Psalm 119:4-6 (KJV)*

My grandma used to say, "Just because a person
does you wrong doesn't mean you do them wrong.
Don't do evil for evil and don't do spite[ful] work. You
do your part, and let God do the rest."

Although it is tempting, reciprocating mistreatment
is not pleasing to God. We become hindrances to God's
promises and blessings when we entertain the desires
and/or engage in attempts to retaliate and try to avenge
ourselves.

Yet, there are times that, when privileged to
information regarding your afflictions or challenges,
many will presume to know what they would do in your

59

position and tell you what you should do or should've done. If you do not do or have never considered or tried what's been suggested, then they will often tell you straightforwardly or imply that you're foolish or naive. I encountered this a great deal when I shared personal experiences. Often, the passion about how I should or should not have reacted or responded came from empathy, disbelief, and concern. Still, I imperfectly—sometimes at peace and other times while having a mental meltdown and looking foolish to my confidants—continued to behave the way I knew God desired.

The scriptures teach that we are to place our trust in God and follow His direction for our lives. Therefore, what presents itself as foolish or naive, I like to call being user-friendly. Those who hurt us will notice that we continue to treat them well and think they are using us or pulling the strings. However, God is the sovereign one! He is our user in that He calls us to act in service to Him, and we submit to being pliable and obedient to His will and His way. God's use of us is not like that of man; His operating, tapping, and switching our mind, heart, and behavioral controls are not exploitive; rather they are restorative, redemptive, and purposed for living out His call. Therefore, in and of God's use, despite afflictions and challenges, we experience solace and peace that discourage acting and/or speaking in ways that others may perceive as justifiable. We speak and behave as God says and demonstrates we should.

When we allow ourselves to be user-friendly, we respect and follow God's commandments, realizing and understanding that we do not conform nor submit to the world's nature and definition regarding use. We are also not ashamed of what God's use of us looks like to anyone because we know bad is for good; brokenness is for building; and weeping is for joy so that He will be glorified!

Thank you, God, for making me more like you—even during times I want to satisfy the world's perspective on what I should do to survive or who I need to become to thrive. Lord, I trust you. Help me always find peace in being who you say I should be and doing what you say I should do. Amen.

Peace Seventeen

I Bet You Won't Come Outside

Come unto me, all ye that labour and are heavy laden,
and I will give you rest.
Matthew 11:28 (KJV)

Growing up, when someone said the words, "I bet you won't come outside," to another person, it was a dare and indirect invitation to engage in a physical fight or other negative confrontation. Those six little words had a powerful meaning for the wrong reasons back then. However, they became an invitation to a faith-fight during my life's most trying times: when I struggled between the desires to quit and to know and experience Jesus and rest.

Leaving my home and city that I loved was challenging in so many ways. It forced me to make unwanted but necessary adjustments because of limited resources and residing a significant distance from my kids' and my usual conveniences. There was also the flooding pain of the realization that I needed connection, but I had spent years isolating, disconnecting, and not cultivating long-term, supportive relationships. Even as I write this entry, I am tearfully experiencing the resurfacing of fears and feelings of abandonment, desertion, and rejection, which have always led to my default response: isolation.

However, this time in isolation, I have felt the Spirit of God nudging me with the words, "I bet you won't come outside"! I have felt and continue to feel Him encouraging me and saying to trust Him and come outside of what holds my potential and me hostage. At times, the words bring me peace. Other times, I feel the agitation of being beckoned from my comfort spaces and false senses of security. Still, I find myself wanting to go!

God is saying to you today, "I bet you won't come outside"! Come outside of your hurtful circumstances, your pain, and shame! Allow your fight to become a faithful one, pursuing and trusting in Him! I bet you won't come outside! Come outside of your brokenness from misuse and abuse. Allow the Lord to mend your heart and make you whole! When you come outside, you surrender to God your physical exertion associated with worry and trying to control your life and relationships. When you come outside, you can have peace and rest because of God's faithfulness to you and His ability to do what you are not equipped to do.

Coming outside and unto God looks like hoping for and having loving relationships in spite of…! Coming outside and unto God looks like living in spite of…!

For me, right now, it also looks like knowing the pain I am having to endure serves a larger purpose than just my feeling sad, angry, and ashamed. It's coming outside of who I wanted that didn't want me. It's making peace with relationships that were one-sided, abandoning, and misleading to establish relationship with a faithful God.

I bet you won't come outside of it all, surrender everything to God, and receive His rest to live!

Dear Lord, my hope is in you. My faith is in you. Your faithfulness is something I do not comprehend but need desperately. Help me to always find peace in coming outside of life's noise and unto you. Amen.

Peace Eighteen

Fix Your Faith

Jesus saith unto him, Thomas, because thou hast seen me, thou hast believed: blessed are they that have not seen, and yet have believed. John 20:29 (KJV)

The last four years of my life have been hard. Life events and the uneventfulness of life have left me devastated. One of the hardest parts has been contending with the realization of oversharing aspects of my life where there was either a lack of listening capacity or a disinterest beyond the scope of gathering and knowing surface information.

Sadly, society has decided, and we have appeared relieved to accept, that helping those who are hurting and sitting with people in suffering are things from which we need protection. More and more, we are being convincingly advised to distance ourselves from people who, "drain," us with their issues in lieu of teachings on how to listen with the ears of Christ, with compassion and empathy, as well as with faith and confidence in His role and ability. It is only in occurrences of outward signs of tragedy that we begin to launch or engage in, "check on your friends and family" efforts. I cannot speak for everyone in my position, but personally I've spoken about my experiences most often when things had been at their darkest and dire. Reaching out was usually a survival attempt stemming from an urgency to disbelieve less of what I was seeing and believe more in what I could not.

For months, after moving back home to my mom's, I did not speak candidly with anyone about the pain I was in and, much like Thomas, I needed proof so that I could believe Jesus is alive. I craved a clear understanding of the meaning of His work in my life that resembled nothing unlike a mess. Does Jesus even care about me? What about my kids; does He care about them? There were times it was even difficult to get out of bed or move from my seat. My mom would call out "Get up! Wash your face, brush your teeth, and comb your hair! We don't know why God allows what He allows or why people do what they do, but we have to take God at His Word no matter what! You may feel down, but take up your mat and walk, and tell God you trust Him!" What she was instructing me to do was not necessarily about improving my outer appearance. She was encouraging me to snap out of my need to *see* to believe; and fix my faith!

We are blessed when we believe without seeing, and those blessings surpass our material needs or desires. Our faith blesses us with wellness in our souls, incomprehensible peace, contentment in God, and strength to keep believing beyond the obvious.

So, without knowing what is next or having any assurance of a desired outcome, get up; fix your face; but most importantly, fix your faith! Believe God's Word, understanding that fixing our faith is not about what we share with people and their responses or lack thereof. It is about sharing with our Creator, the one who listens with grace and knows us and what we are struggling to disbelieve and believe to survive. It's not as simple as looking in the mirror with positive regard and saying nice things to ourselves. Fixing our faith means, during our highs and lows, seeking and being in the presence of God by praying, reading, filling ourselves with His Word, and repeating His truth concerning us! The Word of God can change our outlook into a more positive one that isn't based on what we say or view as our potential. Rather, it is based on who God is, our knowledge of Him, and our unwavering faith in who He is and what He says.

God, I thank you for your word, strength, mercy, and grace that allow me to keep going even when I do not want to or feel I simply cannot. I never want to give up! Grant me peace in my faith-fight to keep believing what you have said and not what I see. Lonely times are hard, Lord, and it's so easy for me to feel

misunderstood and fear abandonment. Reassure me of your presence. Help me to hold fast to my faith, recognize when it needs fixing and fix it in peace! Amen.

Peace Nineteen

Believe God

*Let not your heart be troubled; you believe in God,
believe also in Me. John 14:1 (NKJV)
For he chose us in him before the creation of the
world to be holy and blameless in his sight. In love he
predestined us for adoption to sonship through Jesus
Christ, in accordance with his pleasure and will—"
Ephesians 1:4-5 (NIV)
But now, this is what the LORD says— he who
created you, Jacob, he who formed you, Israel: "Do
not fear, for I have redeemed you; I have summoned
you by name; you are mine. When you pass through
the waters, I will be with you; and when you pass
through the rivers, they will not sweep over you. When
you walk through the fire, you will not be burned; the
flames will not set you ablaze." Isaiah 43:1-2 (NIV)*

It is often said, regarding unhealthy relationships, that we should believe in whom or what people first reveal to us concerning themselves and then manage the relationship accordingly. However, I feel maintaining our belief in God, His love, and His Word is a greater, more favorable, and beneficial charge and assignment.

We are more willing, than not, to believe what is in front of us. We believe what we can see and/or hear, which is why we are emotional and responsive. What we disbelieve are people's audacity and lack of regard for our feelings, the relationship, and who we are and have been to them. Instead of not believing what they have exposed, we do not receive and accept it, and allow them more demonstrations at our expense and sometimes to our detriment. We also disbelieve our position with God and His ability to satisfy us in relationship with Him, as well as supply us with fulfilling, worthy connections. Consequently, we make every effort and take every measure to maintain connections to whom and what fills us with what we are determined to feel.

Relationships can be challenging in ways that leave us physically and emotionally rejected and feeling alone, deserted, and shattered. To cope with and remain in such relationships, we instinctively persuade ourselves to create fantastic alternate versions of people and do not receive and accept who or what they have shown. We try to preserve and heal certain connections so that we do not have to experience a familiar or feared void in our hearts and lives. However, the scriptures affirm that, even before any relational hurts and heartbreaks occurred, God chose us, is with us all the time, redeemed and restored us and, with pleasure, called us His own. What peace we would have if only we believed in *that* relationship and what *He* shows!

Personally, I am not very accepting or receptive of what is often revealed about others nor myself in relationships—especially when it entails some form or degree of letting go. While believing what I am seeing and hearing, I still look for, "meant wells," in instances where I know there were none and do not particularly like myself when I do. Seeing and hearing a person being deceptive, manipulative, offensive, and simply not good to and/or for us, warrants fervent praying to receive and accept his or her messages. Receiving and accepting mean knowing and understanding there is no alternate person, and the experience with him or her really is what it is. When we lack the ability to do that, we, instead, start to receive and accept lies about ourselves based on who we had to become to survive and maintain the relationship. The scriptures affirm God's protection from life's such distresses and trials that cause our hearts to be troubled when we place our belief in Him—where it belongs.

Regardless of what the world may show, it is God we must believe and in who He shows and tells us *He* is. We do not need to get muddled and distracted in attempts to discern people's modes of operation or what to believe and not believe about them. Receive and accept their messages, but turn to God—always.

Believe Him! Believe what His Word says! There is no alternate version of God nor His Word and truth, and we do not have to create one to have or remain in relationship.

*Dear God, thank you for who your Word says I am to you and who you are to me! I trust you. I believe you; I believe **in** you. I count on you. I need peace in receiving and accepting who people show me they are. Help me to have peace in believing what you say, do, and your ability to fill every void in my life. Amen.*

Peace Twenty

Following Through

The steps of a good man are ordered by the Lord: and he delighteth in his way. Though he fall, he shall not be utterly cast down: for the Lord upholdeth him with his hand. Psalm 37: 23-24 (KJV)

One of the challenges I encountered as a teacher was convincing students of the importance of following through with directions and instructions. I say, "following through," because they knew how to follow them but would only do so to a certain degree of understanding or upon reaching a particular section of their work. Often, students who started strong would demonstrate an inability to maintain that same or a comparable momentum through to completion of tests or assignments. The closer they were to finishing, the more their mistakes— usually repetitive—would build.

Although I would advise them to look back at the instructions and other questions to make certain they were staying on track, some students simply were not inclined to comply—even as examples became more challenging. If only they had re-read the instructions or referred to what they had previously done to get to their present level of questioning, then they would have known what to do, as well as what not to do.

Like my students, we also, at times, do not refer to and follow through on God's direction and instructions. Scripture tells us that God orders a good man's steps. In other words, when we desire to walk in the ways of the Lord, He directs, instructs, and disciplines our steps, while remaining faithful through our seasons of development and learning to abide in Him. God advises us on the best choices and decisions; He mercifully assists us in navigating the opportunities and options we freely choose; and He gifts us conviction, compassion, and forgiveness to proceed and live with them. Because God knows we are susceptible to sin and poor and selfish choices, He comforts and supports us with His unwavering hand. In His Word, He has provided correctives, so we do not remain in the conditions or circumstances of our choices nor bound to a course and pattern of repeated mistakes and missteps.

Just as the levels of questioning in my students' work became increasingly difficult and required the acquisition and use of new and prior knowledge, so do certain challenges or problems in various and specific areas of our lives require the acknowledgment of our past and present actions and God's proven faithfulness. It is imperative to look to God, follow-up, and follow through. In doing so, we can recall, re-examine, and reflect upon the steps that got us where we are. We can also realize and access His grace and guidance to recover and improve our steps forward.

God, thank you for peace in knowing that you remain. Lord, help me be at peace with your guidance that steers me toward you and following through in your order. Amen.

Peace Twenty-One

Send it Back

*Those who live according to the flesh have their minds
set on what the flesh desires; but those who live in
accordance with the Spirit have their minds set on
what the Spirit desires. The mind governed by the
flesh is death, but the mind governed by the Spirit is
life and peace. The mind governed by the flesh is
hostile to God; it does not submit to God's law, nor
can it do so. Those who are in the realm of the flesh
cannot please God. Romans 8:5-8 (NIV)*

I think some of the worst feedback I received, during
challenging times, left me feeling the way I was healing
was wrong and like my small steps—although giant to
me—were not enough. True to form, I would either
attempt to explain myself, or end the conversation, and
spiral into depression, self-loathing, and self-criticism.

My grandmother would always tell us that there was
no harm in listening if someone was telling you
something good, meaning what is right and the
importance of doing the right things. She would
sometimes warn us, however, that there are some
people who will tell you anything. The message I

receive from her words, in this season of my life, is that all advice is not always intended for or necessarily conscious of me. Some, while practical or sound, may not be the advice fit for my current environment, where I am in my grief and hurt, nor where I am on my healing journey. Other advice, simply lacking in wisdom and good judgment, may assault my character. While it might be suitable for the person advising me, it's not advice characteristic of who I am and who God has called me to be.

Scripture advises us to act according to the Spirit and not the flesh. While fleshly advice may give us the temporary satisfaction of knowing we have gotten vengeance either in words or actions, it does not bring us life and peace. Therefore, we must send it back! This means asking God to remove it from our thoughts and not allowing any part of ourselves to absorb or retain it.

It is not easy to forego our "pound of another's flesh" and choose the ways of God—especially when our wounds and brokenness are fresh. At first, payback thoughts and advice can seem appealing; however, we must send them back by seeking God more earnestly and relentlessly! Go after the Spirit! Choose the things of God: love, peace, mercy, grace, and forgiveness. Send anything else back! Set aside pride that feeds the need to retaliate, and submit to trusting and believing in God's help, guidance, comfort, and healing.

Dear God, help me not to act or speak in ways that are vengeful against people who have hurt me. Help me to recognize and send back advice that will keep me existing in pieces instead of living in peace. Amen.

Peace Twenty-Two

Handle with Care

Do you not know that your bodies are temples of the Holy Spirit, who is in you, whom you have received from God? You are not your own; you were bought at a price. Therefore honor God with your bodies.
1 Corinthians 6:19-20 (NIV)

We experience difficulties in life and often think they are due to something either wrong within or about us. Many of us default to self-harming behaviors because we feel the need to control something we cannot, or we have allowed circumstances, experiences, or people to dictate how we feel and care for ourselves. Although self-destructive, our default behaviors provide a sense of peace that is false and temporary, but also genuinely satisfying.

For me, that has meant using food to cope with traumatic experiences and distress caused by strained or neglectful relationships. Since I was a young adult, I have struggled with what I call a disordered, dysfunctional, and unhealthy relationship with food, usually stirred by negative emotions. It has been a comfort in loneliness; punishment when I felt I should have been smarter, more aware, or vocal; and a suppressor of anxious thoughts and feelings. In either case, I would consume excessive amounts of sugary and salty food combinations until tired and only able to sleep. For several days following, I would drink a considerable amount of water throughout the day and restrict certain foods and calories. Time after time, in an emotional whirlwind, I exercised this routine of abuse, only to awaken to no real sense of peace and the realization that abusing my body had changed nothing that was happening in my life.

It can be wearisome and challenging for us to truly love and appreciate ourselves without the knowledge and understanding of who and whose we are. Scripture tells us that our bodies belong to God. For them, He made and paid the ultimate sacrifice and price. When we consider it this way, we are in use of what belongs to Him—like being in use of someone else's car. Because it is not ours, we would be deliberate with its care and mindful of its condition, prior to use and upon returning it. The same should be true for our bodies. We should want to take care of them mentally, physically, and not dishonor them by submitting ourselves to sin, destructive behaviors, or ungodly temptations and desires.

This is not easy, and I still struggle with food abuse. However, each day, I am learning to accept that I do not belong to myself nor the people and circumstances triggering emotions that make me feel abusing myself with food is the answer. I belong to God and, just as I would intentionally and cautiously manage the care and condition of anything else that does not belong to me, I should, and you should, handle these bodies—His bodies—with care!

Dear God, help me to be at peace with what I can't control, knowing that you care for me even when others or I do not. I know that I am not my own. Help me to find peace in handling myself honorably because I belong to you! Amen.

Peace Twenty-Three

A Presence Change

*No one sews a piece of unshrunk cloth on an old
garment; or else the new piece pulls away from the
old, and the tear is made worse. And no one puts new
wine into old wineskins; or else the new wine bursts
the wineskins, the wine is spilled, and the wineskins
are ruined. But new wine must be put into new
wineskins. Mark 2:21-22 (NKJV)*

Some of the most emotionally unsettling and
disruptive words we can either hear from or say to
individuals we are in any relationship with are: "That's
just the way I am." I always tell my son and daughter,
"No one remains unchanged even when both of you are
unwilling." What I am trying to help them understand
is, we are changed in some way— if only in knowledge
or thinking —just from our interactions and exchanges
with others. The same is true when we experience the
presence of God. Whether we receive Him or not, we
are changed because we cannot undo the experience of
His presence, nor can we "un-know" the witnessing or
testament His presence permits.

The scriptures explain that new wine added to old bottles causes the bottles to break and wine to spill, and new cloth sewn onto older, worn cloth further weakens and tears the fabric. Similarly, in relationships where only one person is either willing or unwilling to change, or alter and adjust thinking and behaviors, it threatens the well-being of everyone involved and can further devastate their current conditions, as well as the state of the relationship.

Jesus' response to the Pharisees was about change. Unlike the Pharisees, the disciples were not fasting because they were in His presence. In the presence of Christ, there is newness of grace and mercy. They did not need to be as they always were or bound to religious acts ordinarily done in His physical absence.

Experiencing God's presence is not intended for the preserving, replenishing, or reviving of our former selves. Believing and operating as if that is the case, is damaging and a disservice to others as well as ourselves. For our relationships to grow and remain strong, we must make peace with neither expecting nor accepting the maintenance or refill of who we or another individual has always been.

When God renews, changes, and transforms us, He fills us with new grace, mercy, and peace that release us from remaining who we have always been and doing what we have always done. Our routine thoughts and actions become disqualified. Therefore, in His presence—no matter the exchange or our reception or acceptance—none of us can remain as we were.

Dear Lord, you call us to newness to fill us there. Strengthen me to remain at peace with change that allows me to be open to experiencing you and all that you desire for my life and loved ones. Amen.

Peace Twenty-Four

Real Power is Willed Power

*Now therefore be not grieved, nor angry with
yourselves, that ye sold me hither: for God did send
me before you to preserve life. And God sent me
before you to preserve you a posterity in the earth,
and to save your lives by a great deliverance.*
Genesis 45:5, 7 (KJV)

The scripture references Joseph's conversation with
his brothers whose jealousy caused them to throw him
in a pit, leave him to die, and then decide to get him out
and sell him into slavery. Despite their actions, when
Joseph has an opportunity to get revenge, he
acknowledges and obeys the will of God. He informs
his brothers that he is there to help and save them from
the coming famine.

When people hurt us, we can sometimes feel there
is no greater demonstration and expression of God's
favor or power in our lives than our gaining the upper
hand or advantage where they are concerned. Although
Joseph endured violent and spiteful suffering because
of his brothers' envy and cruelty, he also received God's

protection and provision which restored and repositioned him to make them suffer as he had. Instead of getting revenge, Joseph chose to exercise his real power which is willed power or acting in the will of God.

So many days and nights, I ruminated over chaotic thoughts and self-insults because I did not use my position of advantage to make others feel the reciprocal pain of loneliness, fear of the unknown, self-shaming and blaming, and fear of abandonment resulting from their silent treatment and indifference. Yet, I know it was God speaking to me through sermons, music, and scriptures, instructing me to remain in His will for power to heal, maintain peace, and not self-destruct.

When we access and use the power of God's will, we do not allow the actions or inactions of others to cause us to dismantle our authentic selves and character. Who we truly are is in God's Word and will—not who we tell ourselves we are and how we define ourselves based on who or what life may condition us to believe.

Acting in willed power is not a matter of our own strength but a matter of relinquishing our perceptions, feelings, and abilities to God's will. It involves allowing His might and power to be our defense, guide our actions, temper our thoughts and emotions, and soften our words and speech. Acting in the power of

His will is understanding that God also desires healing and freedom from brokenness and sin for our offenders. God's willed power is the power in which Joseph had the ability to make peace with his brothers and free them of their sadness and anger with themselves for what they had done to him.

Possessing *real* power does not require us to secure or exercise an obvious advantage, nor is it best evidenced by our ability to execute retaliatory acts. Real power is having peace in speaking and acting in alignment with God's character and sovereign plan revealed in His instructions and examples of how we should live. God's will *is* the power! Real power is willed power!

Dear Lord, thank you for your willed power! Thank you for teaching me that I am not what was done to me or what I have done to others. Strengthen me each day to have peace in speaking and acting according to your will. Amen.

Peace Twenty-Five

When It's Good

Being confident of this very thing, that he which hath begun a good work in you will perform it until the day of Jesus Christ: Philippians 1:6 (KJV)

Paul is assuring the Philippians that God is both savior and sanctifier. God will not leave them, nor will He stop working as they walk the path of what He began. He will not stop until their work and they come into agreement and alignment with the truth and character of Christ—on the day of Christ! This is also true for us. God began His work before we even had knowledge of our existence and, although life's challenges make it otherwise appear, He is yet working.

I am a graduate student studying marriage and family therapy. As part of one of my course requirements, I had to work within a group that met weekly. For one of our meetings, our professor scheduled a group observation and evaluation. Each of us would be displaying our counseling skills in practice.

Prior to our meeting and observation that day, I struggled and battled various issues internally. My mind was flooded with self-doubt, and I questioned, "How did I get here"? What initially felt like a calling was starting to feel burdensome with its offerings of new experiences ripping me from isolated comfort. I could not quiet my mind of my heart's questions: "I need this, but what if I fail? What if my professor does not truly see me? What if she does not understand? What will I do if I am unable to convey my desire to help?" Worried, tired, and overwhelmed, I was convinced this program's particular obligation would be just another act and scene in the dramatic tragicomedy I called my life. What, on earth, could I say or do to help married couples and families when my own marriage had failed and altered the lives of my children? I simply wanted to quit! I emailed my professor expressing this and told her I was only attending the meeting because I didn't want to let my team down. She sent an encouraging email response that ended, "Remember, if it's not good, then He's not done."

A month later, I saw a social media post celebrating the song, "Joy in the Morning." I unmuted the post to hear voices singing, "If it's not good, then He's not done." Filled with excitement, I opened and searched my music app and downloaded the song. The best part was being able to share it with my son and encourage him as well.

It is important that we believe and embrace the Word of God, knowing that He will not stop what He has begun in us until completion. Although we may never understand what went wrong in our lives or know why certain things had to happen to us, we can find and experience peace from Paul's reminder of God's promise. We can rest assured that even the bad things are being used to steadily build us into God's original design. God is working to restore us with His grace and might, and He is establishing our character as one that is more like His. He is perfecting us in this world while proving we are apart from it and will not stop until the coming of Christ—when it is good! We need to only believe, trust, and remain in a faithful relationship with Him.

God, thank you for not stopping your work even when I am doubtful and stop doing my part. Help me each day to see my life as filled with opportunities to find peace, to desire and acquire more of you, and to become more like you. Thank you for your promise to finish what you start! Thank you for not leaving me in life's pieces. Amen.

Peace Twenty-Six

Free

And ye shall know the truth, and the truth shall make you free. John 8:32 (KJV)

I recall a therapy session with my then therapist of three years, during which we reflected on my growth since my initial visit. I heaved a long, uncomfortable sigh at the thought of that first visit. I was a wreck—crying uncontrollably and certain nothing I was saying was coherent. At that time, there was such an urgency and desperation in my whole body to know if my mind and heart were deceiving me. I yearned to know whether my relational needs and wants were normal or just impairments and dysfunctions that authored my darkest moments and deepest betrayals. When he asked me how I felt about everything now, I could not find any word or words to express what I felt. I could only tell him what I thought I was expected to feel—what I knew certain people in my life wanted me to feel: *free*.

That was a lie. Nothing I had learned—nothing at all—had made me feel free! Instead, everything sorted and uncovered in therapy felt like added suffering due to my sudden loss of a quite blissful ignorance—a loss that sadly kept me bound by depression and anxiety more than ever!

Our sometimes-haphazard use of the scripture to suggest there is freedom in any context of telling the truth is a misapplication—mostly without malicious intent—of what God's Word means concerning truth and freedom. We tell people, "The truth shall set you free," when we suspect they are being deceptive about eating leftovers we waited all day to eat or about borrowing our possessions without permission. Yet the scripture's concepts of freedom and truth are much deeper. Jesus is telling the people that freedom is in the truth that is Him. We are set free from the world's contextual truths and freedoms when we know and believe in God; believe He is who He says He is; and believe, have faith, and trust in His Word and works.

While it may offer relief from feelings of guilt or resolve internal and external conflicts, finding freedom in Christ is not about persuading someone to clear his or her conscience about leftovers and possessions, nor is it about us learning the truth about our relationships and our place and value concerning them. Freedom is about being in the presence of God and in confession, commitment, and connection with Him! We receive God's gift of freedom when our image of Him remains intact regardless of what circumstances reveal! When we remain in pursuit of knowledge and understanding

of God, His Word, promises, and faithfulness, we can become free! God sets us free with the teachings and discerning power of the Holy Spirit; His unfailing love; and His uncompromising gifts of grace, mercy, healing, and purpose…I could go on! Professing freedom in God brings me peace!

Truths about my life and myself discovered in therapy were helpful to know, yet knowledge alone brought me no freedom or peace and, honestly, deeply grieved me. It has been, and still is, the truth of who God is, in the muck of it all with me, that frees me daily!

Dear God, I desire more of you. In you, there is peace I need when the knowledge of who I am in the lives of others distresses me, or knowledge of my ailments and the conditions of my surroundings sadden me. Enable me to seek and understand more about who you are, who I am in you, and allow your spirit, presence, will, mercy, and healing power to set me free! Amen.

Peace Twenty-Seven

Storms

Be strong and of good courage, do not fear nor be afraid of them; for the Lord your God, He is the One who goes with you. He will not leave you nor forsake you. Deuteronomy 31:6 (NKJV)
I will praise the Lord according to his righteousness: and will sing praise to the name of the Lord most high. Psalm 7:17 (KJV)

A critical, often innocent, mistake parents or family members can make is projecting their fears onto children. When I became a mom, I discovered this was not only necessary but difficult to avoid. Although there is an 11-year age gap between my son and daughter, it's been beneficial to sit with them individually and collectively to discuss their fears without focusing on my own. I have learned to acknowledge the validity of their fears, as well as the enormity of their sources, while maintaining my composure and preserving my inner hysterics for when I'm alone.

On the first Tuesday of 2023, we awakened to rain and howling winds. My daughter was frightened and in tears. I got into bed with her, held her close, and asked what was making her so scared. She told me she was afraid of a tornado and that something bad might happen to us.

Pangs of guilt pierced my heart and burnt my skin and bones. I did this. I could not find a better option between staying and letting go but could only weigh the pros and cons to determine which option was less unbearable. I took her from her home where she was usually playing on the basement level and missed storm activity. Now, here, in my mom's home, with a different layout, she was having a too-close-for-comfort storm experience. I resisted the urge to cry too, but I felt her with everything in me. I felt her fear and longing but knew I needed to spare her that. She needed me to share what God had been teaching me in this season: He is the great *I Am*. Nothing about this world changes God's love and grace. When scripture says He won't forsake or fail us, it's because it is not possible! God's righteousness is that He doesn't flip His script to accommodate circumstances. He remains God of our hope and the source of all we need—even in storms!

I began to say that to my daughter. I reminded her of our sudden move: the people, things, pieces, and *peaces* each of us left behind. Then, I reassured her that after all the things God protected our minds, hearts, and bodies from, He was not about to leave us now! We praised God for His power in the wind and rain which serve as reminders that He is in control! We thanked God for His shifts in His creation we are permitted to experience and witness. They affirm that He governs all life's storms, and it doesn't matter their force or turbulence; our great, unfailing God is with us!

She stopped crying, and we noticed sunlight peeking through the blinds. The storm had passed, and we thanked and praised God some more!

Life is filled with scary storms. The rains and winds of trials and hurts disrupt our peace and often test and attack our faith. We are left questioning whether God has left or forgotten us and fear we will suffer pain or harm. However, the scriptures tell us that we do not have to fear. We are neither abandoned nor left to the devices of any storm we must withstand because we have the assurance that God will be with us! Praise Him!

Thank you, God, for peace in storms! Thank you for the truth and righteousness of your promises. Help me to keep them in my heart through every storm experience. Amen.

Peace Twenty-Eight

Can't See for Looking

*Can any hide himself in secret places that I shall not
see him? saith the Lord. Do not I fill heaven and
earth? saith the Lord. Jeremiah 23:24 (KJV)
The Lord is nigh unto them that are of a broken heart;
and saveth such as be of a contrite spirit.
Psalm 34:18 (KJV)*

The first trip I made back to the city where I had left
many pieces and *peaces* was a difficult one. Once I
approached my former exit, knowing there was no
other way to my destination than past my former home,
I was overcome with anger and hurt. I must have looked
insane to other drivers at stoplights because I was
obviously in the car alone; yet, I was crying, screaming,
and clearly having a heated conversation. I kept
pounding my fist on the steering wheel while asking
God, "Where are you?" I demanded to know why He
was not showing up for my kids since He appeared to
have no interest in showing up for me! It just did not
seem fair, and I could not comprehend why He was not
present with me, like I had witnessed what had to be
His presence with others. I arrived thirty minutes early

for my appointment, which was just enough time for me to park, recline my seat, curl up in a fetal position, and weep. Over and over, I kept asking, "God, where are you?"

I have an uncle who says, "You can't see for looking," whenever he sees you looking for something that is clearly visible, but you still do not see it. A preoccupation with the process of searching or a fixation on the fact that what you seek is not where you placed it or anticipated it would be, makes what you're looking for impossible to see—even when it's right in front of you.

That incident in my car happened over a year ago. I needed so badly to know where God was and why He wasn't attending to my pain. I was looking for Him when the scriptures tell His exact location. My heart was broken, and scripture says that He's near the broken-hearted. I was demanding that He show Himself, in my life, and scripture says that His presence fills heaven and earth. He was right there and always had been. I couldn't see for looking. I will go even further and say that, during that time in my life, I couldn't hear for listening either!

That's the way it is sometimes. We are deep in despair and, God, from whom we cannot hide and who fills every space and place of His creation, has said that He is near. However, we do not see Him, and we question His presence because we're looking for Him to show up the way we need things to happen and according to our plans. We do not hear Him speaking to us because we're listening for Him to say something that we want to hear and that supports our agenda.

As I am still navigating peace, I am also working on seeing and hearing—not merely looking for what I want to see and listening for what I want to hear. If I am honest, every time suicidal thoughts and ideations didn't prevail, I know it's because God was right there. Every time "something" told me not to respond a certain way, I know it was His voice. I couldn't see or hear Him then because I simply wanted God to stop imposing His plans for me that did not correspond with or look like what I planned for myself. God just wouldn't let me have my way!

Consider such times in your own life when, in spite of it all, you didn't give up or give in. You made it! He kept you here! God is concerned about you and whatever and whomever concerns you. He has not left you. He is with you—if you would only stop looking and see!

Lord, thank you for protection and care. Thank you for keeping my heart and mind when times have been hardest. Forgive me when I don't acknowledge your love, grace, and mercy because I'm looking and listening for things to appear and sound as I want. Thank you for the peace of your presence. Amen.

Peace Twenty-Nine

Tired Faith

*My flesh and my heart fail; But God is the strength of
my heart and my portion forever.*
Psalm 73:26 (NKJV)
*That your faith should not stand in the wisdom of men,
but in the power of God. 1 Corinthians 2:5 (KJV)*

About two months prior to my daughter being
referred and scheduled to see a neurological
ophthalmologist, I was told by my ophthalmologist that
my eyes showed signs of stress, associated with a
condition known as central serous retinopathy. We
looked over my eye-scan images, and he explained that
if I could not manage my stress levels, I would
temporarily lose sight in my right eye. The rest of what
he said sounded muddled. I could only hear my internal
voice scolding how foolish I had been to allow the
stress of my marital and familial states to further harm
my health and threaten my well-being.

The time after my visit and preceding my daughter's
appointment was hard. "Lord," I would cry, "How can
I not be stressed? What if she's not okay? Help me
control my 'mom-thoughts'!" I knew I needed to get a

handle on my stress, but I was stressed trying to control my stress and stressed constantly wondering if my efforts were working. I was praying—I had **been** praying—but now I was questioning if I was even doing it right.

Her appointment day arrived and, after three hours of subjecting her to tiring questions, tests, and waits, the doctor told me her eyes were healthy and there were no further concerns or additional tests required. The relief and gratitude I felt could only be expressed in praise!

Even with the good news, the drive back to my mom's house seemed longer and more exhausting than usual. I could not help but wonder what my concern for my daughter, during the months waiting for her appointment and the actual appointment experience, had done to my eyesight.

That evening, I was sitting down to eat and looked up at my mom, who had just walked into the kitchen and, fighting back my tears, I said, "I'm tired."

The beauty and comfort of the scriptures are in their evidence that God knew we would get tired on life's journey. He knew that our bodies would be exhausted, our hearts would feel discouraged, and we would become believers struggling with tired faith in and under the wait and weight of our circumstances. The scriptures also remind us that He is the strength in our bodies and the encouragement our hearts need when our faith is tired. God is always enough and more of what we need when we need it —forever. Men may be wise; however, tired faith will not be restored by their wisdom. God restores tired faith and, once it is restored, it has the power of withstanding that can only come from the power of God.

Whatever has our faith tired: believing but tired of trying; believing but weary in well-doing; believing but disconnected, sick, sad, or anxious and hurt; it is all right to fall on Him. It doesn't matter where our tired faith causes us to fall, because the comfort, strength, and restorative power of God are always near.

Dear Lord, thank you for being all I need. Thank you for moments of tired faith that bring me closer to you, where I can appreciate and abide in peace and rest in your everlasting embrace. Amen.

Peace Thirty

Let Her Go

Do not remember the former things, Nor consider the things of old. Behold, I will do a new thing, Now it shall spring forth; Shall you not know it? I will even make a road in the wilderness And rivers in the desert. Isaiah 43:18-19 (NKJV)

Most nights during the COVID-19 pandemic lockdown, I could not sleep until just before morning. I felt as though I was in a constant state of physical, mental, and emotional distress and exhaustion. The state of my marriage, the state of the world, and the devastation of both gnawed at my core and left me feeling sick with emptiness and worry daily. It was a time I struggled most with staying alive: fearing both dying and living. My mind would constantly run rampant with if-only-then thoughts.

It was also during this time I discovered that shower cries are the best! Water, blended with my tears, cleansed my face as it outpoured all the hurt. I would cry in the shower when my pain was deep and intense, and I had no more words to say to God, who loves me so much, about how unloved, rejected, and neglected I was feeling. Although I felt I could say nothing to Him, I still believed God was hearing everything. Shower cries also yielded pivotal moments that I could hear God as well. It was during a shower cry, incredibly overwhelmed and exhausted by the desperate need for a change of heart and course, I heard Him say, "Let her go"!

Every day, I had been running on this hamster wheel, recollecting the girl I was and how different choices might have improved or made a significant difference in the woman I became. Yet God was telling me to move along and let her go. Focusing on the past, wondering incessantly who I could have been, would not bring me any peace nor was it productive. He wanted me to let her go because we didn't need her for what He was fulfilling in my life at present or would reveal and grant me access to in the future.

Scripture advises us not to focus on what is past, or we will miss the ways God is currently working, as well as the good things ahead. God assures us that, even in what seems like the worst of situations and most unrecoverable of conditions (the wildernesses and deserts), He has made provisions to bring us through. His work in us, regarding His will and purpose for our lives, does not stop where we have left ourselves abandoned and safe-housed because of hurtful circumstances and sins.

Do you ever find yourself looking back and thinking of what you missed, who you could've been, or contemplating: if only…, then...? Let that person go! God is doing something new in you and for you. His forgiveness, healing, provisions, and blessings did not end with that version of you, so let go, and move along in Christ!

Dear Lord, I am grateful to be able to hear your voice. Keep me aware and at peace with what is present. Thank you for not leaving me where I left myself. Amen.

Peace Thirty-One

Let God Time You

But do not forget this one thing, dear friends: With the Lord a day is like a thousand years, and a thousand years are like a day. The Lord is not slow in keeping his promise, as some understand slowness. Instead he is patient with you, not wanting anyone to perish, but everyone to come to repentance. 2 Peter 3:8-9 (NIV)

It can be difficult to maneuver through life's unexpected transitions and issues and even harder to manage and move forward once we are on the other side of them. Both being at peace with healing and healing in peace depend on what we are able and willing to receive and make committed efforts toward.

In 2015, I reconnected with a former college roommate. I had not seen her since she was one of my bridesmaids, and we had only spoken once in 19 years prior to reconnecting. We laughed and shared as though no time had been lost.

As my life's circumstances became increasingly challenging, she would often surprise me with a small gift or card with heartwarming, encouraging words. Once, she sent two bracelets, both with engravings and instructions on when they were to be worn. The first one could be worn immediately and was engraved, "With brave wings she flies". The second one engraved, "Be still and know…," could be worn once I had started my healing journey.

I wanted to change the wearing order. My understanding of my current circumstances conveyed an immediate need of calm and the assurance of God's presence while in the hurt and pain. Brave wings would be more appropriate for later: once I felt I had gotten through it all, and my heart and I were finally ready and able to go on. However, I wore them as instructed and learned…

Brave wings were necessary in the thick of my emotional, mental, and physical distresses. They represented the strength I needed at that time to survive and meant that I would, indeed, survive. They also symbolized my willingness to persevere with joy and contentment through what had become robotic and routine, while having faith in God's authority.

For months preceding my 48th birthday, I was most tortured by thoughts of what was next and if it was too late to achieve my goals, find love, and be loved the way I'd always hoped and prayed. I began wearing the second bracelet shortly after my birthday. Its engraving, "Be still and know," was consistent with this period of my journey that required embracing the quiet and calm of God's pace and timing, while learning to rest in the assurance that He is God!

On the other side of our pain are newfound desires, concerns, and often additional feelings of anger and frustration over what was lost and what remains. Subsequent questions can then start to overwhelm us about what God will do; if He will do it; and how long it will take. The scripture reminds us that God does not operate on our time nor how we process or perceive time's passing. He will keep His promises but not according to our timing or vision. God will execute His will by His authority, and He will remain faithful to His Word and us when we arrive at His destination and are ready.

It's not too late. God's lovingkindness is permanent sustenance under the conditions of sin and fallenness and in the chaos of intense emotional pain and doubts. We can always trust the wait on God—He is worthy! God will guide us through life's hardships and show us His way to repentance, redemption, restoration, and peace. Be still and know that God is timing you and your arrival to where, whom, and what He has prepared. There is no better or more patient timekeeper!

God, thank you for your patience and the peace of your timing! Thank you for all the ways you consider me in keeping your promises. You know when I am ready. Lord, help me to be patient. Help me to be still, believe, and trust. Amen.

Peace Thirty-Two

Let Whys Die

I will instruct you and teach you in the way you should go; I will counsel you with my loving eye on you. Psalm 32:8 (NIV)

For one of my graduate courses, I had to complete a journal assignment about three experiences: one thrilling, another amazing, and a final one sobering. When I saw the assignment, I was immediately saddened. This was not the first course or assignment requiring that I recall and discuss times in my life that I would rather not. Immediately, it surfaced—that word—the single-word question. Yet, I refused to ask it. Finding *peaces of me* no longer permitted that ask!

My thrilling and amazing experiences both preceded and were deeply, painfully impacted by my sobering one. I was both thrilled and amazed that I married my high school sweetheart and became a mom twice, with no PCOS (polycystic ovarian syndrome) complications, only to become sobered by the disruptive dysfunction of my family dynamic and its faulty foundation that had caused a slow, agonizing, but abrupt and logical break.

An inconsistent paternal presence accompanied by fallenness, weakness, and the sickness of addictions had prepared me. It was a broken, impaired presence, and its inability to see me as a little girl, and not a mere pretty, accessible object, and prey, had primed my heart's condition to give blindly what it craved. Sadly, just as I was that little girl, I have too often been the lost, desperate woman, begging the question—just one word—although small, requiring so much and so many answers: "Why"?

God knows the extensions of our whys. Why is this happening to me? Why am I not further in life? Why don't I have...? Why can't I be...? Why?" However, God does not always answer our whys the way we prefer—if at all.

I still don't have answers to whys concerning many of my paternal and marital circumstances. However, I am more at peace than I have been since asking on that cold Saturday morning when the little girl was robbed. I am also more at peace than on that, also cold, Wednesday morning the woman was stripped of the only reality she'd known and forced to start anew. My peace comes from knowing, as the scripture says, that God's loving eye is on me. It's on all of us! He sees and understands everything about us that we cannot. We just need to let our whys die and trust Him. During our why moments and questioning, God is lovingly developing us in areas that need more of Him. He is changing our desires, how we see ourselves, and our lives to align with Him, His design, Word, and promises.

When you are hurting, let your whys die to what God is teaching; what He is instructing and where His counsel is steering your faith. When you're lonesome, sick, or lost, allow your whys to die to what a friend; what a counselor; what a redeemer; and what a healer our faithful God is!

Experiences have taught me that sometimes people simply do hurtful things and do not understand why or cannot explain the nature and origin of their behaviors. In kind, *we* also do things and behave in ways that we are unable to understand or explain. Faith and experience are still teaching me that it is important not to become hindered by or entangled in longing to know "why" and miss God.

Learning and earning what God desires for us, what he expects from us, and where He is leading mean allowing whys to die. When you desire to know why, but peace says "No," consider Doris Aker's hymn, "Lead Me, Guide Me," and its refrain:

"Lead me, guide me along the way,
For if you lead me, I cannot stray.
Lord, let me walk each day with thee.

Lead me, O Lord, lead me."

Lord, in you I have peace in not knowing why. I desire to know what you need from me and what I should learn. Lead me; guide me; I put my faith and trust in you. Amen.

Peace Thirty-Three

God Knows and That's What Matters

The Lord will fight for you, and you shall hold your peace. Exodus 14:14 (NKJV)

During various stages growing up, there were many instances where I could not understand the personalities of my grandmother and mother. Both were quiet, reserved, and showed an unusual amount of self-control and peacefulness during tough times or when facing people's malicious actions and harsh words. My grandmother would say, "God knows, and that's what matters."

My young mind could not process that, nor did it have the desire. I remember being around 26 years-old, when I stood at the church's altar one Sunday for prayer, and one of the ministers came over, placed his hand on my head, and shockingly said, "You will not be like your mother and grandmother." Well, that was music to my ears! It was confirmation that I was never going to forsake my voice for anyone or allow someone to silence me.

When I experienced or witnessed someone being offensive or hurtful, I had little regard for that person's peace and absolutely no interest in rewarding him or her with my silence. I was sensitive and easily affected by disrespect and disappointment. Try as I would to keep quiet, I had to speak my mind. I would never consent to mistreatment by being passive. Because I was most obsessed with establishing everything I would not accept, I was completely oblivious when I was sadly accepting those very things and repeatedly doing so.

Looking back on the last 20 years, I realize that my voice cost me. It cost me time, my health, sleep, and much more. The greatest costs were my relationship with God, being able to hear Him, and having His peace. By giving people's actions or inactions no peace, I forfeited my own. I was so determined I wouldn't become like my mother and grandmother that I didn't see the minister's words were true…just not how I had understood them. I endured some of their same adversities in life and relationships and, just as the minister had spoken, I was nothing like them. What I saw as them being doormats was actually them allowing God—the champion fighter and the one always certain to win—to do their fighting. Their silence was not them forsaking their voices or allowing their voices to be taken. They were maintaining their peace and trusting God to fight for them as the scripture says. I used my voice incorrectly until God began to silence me by requiring that I become someone I didn't want to be, so I could be who He needed me to be.

In the last five years, my fight to overcome anger, resentment, and survive painful seasons of loss and disappointment has looked completely different from what all the hurt made me feel or who it tasked me to become. So many times, I disliked, scolded, and verbally shamed and insulted myself because I wished my fight looked like an actual fight—or at least like one I was winning. Instead, words escaped me when I thought I should've been speaking. Tears flowed and silent cries out to God overwhelmed me when I felt I should've been screaming. I felt love, compassion, and concern when I knew I should've been distant, unmoved, and removed. My grandmother's words would frequently resound in my ears and mind, and God's knowledge of all things started to matter more to me than telling my side, making myself clear, or having my say.

God quiets us when we can't and won't quiet ourselves. It is His way of granting us grace and mercy to see that He always has and will continue to fight for us. God knows, and that's what matters.

Dear Lord, thank you for newfound peace. Thank you for the quietness of your fight. Thank you for helping me to see that you fight best and will fight for me. Amen.

Peace Thirty-Four

You Say That Like It's a Bad Thing

Do not be deceived, God is not mocked; for whatever a man sows, that he will also reap. For he who sows to his flesh will of the flesh reap corruption, but he who sows to the Spirit will of the Spirit reap everlasting life. And let us not grow weary while doing good, for in due season we shall reap if we do not lose heart. Galatians 6:7-9 (NKJV)

Although not usually talked about as a form of abuse, spiritual abuse occurs in familial and social relationships as well as religious communities and organizations. It is sneaky in that it presents itself as care and concern; however, the motive is neither conviction nor correction but condemnation, manipulation, and control. Scriptures are quoted and used, in specific instances and ways, to bind a person to false loyalty and senses of security in individuals who only value the purpose that person serves and his or her willingness and ability to serve or comply.

I never felt such an urgency to master a stage of life quicker than when I became a mom the first time. Every cooperative decision made, or boundary set, to manage asthma and food and environmental allergies, for the safety and well-being of this precious life, was challenged by affinal influences that used scripture discouragingly, often warning, "You're gonna reap what you sow." Inwardly, I would scream, "You say that like it's a bad thing!"

The verses are not one-sided; however, my experience with their paraphrasing was never uplifting and always left me feeling threatened that God was just lying in wait to get me. I was often anxious and second or third-guessing my every word or move. After pursuing an understanding of the actual scripture to completion and in context, I soon realized that I could also have been told, but never was, "You're a loving, attentive mom, and you're going to reap what you sow!"

When it comes to God's Word, great care should be taken to not use it as thoughtless utterances and cause our brothers and sisters to question God's love and wonder if he feels contempt and disdain for them. Clarity of the Word is critical to communicating and carrying out His mission. As people of God, it is important that we encourage one another in the Lord to read, pray, and establish, for ourselves, relationship, knowledge and understanding. When God's people truly believe in the law of sowing and reaping, they do not weaponize Him to hurt, manipulate, and control others or damage their image of Him.

Despite my desire to rush through that new-mom experience, I am grateful to God that His provision, both then and now, has made it impossible for me to miss a single moment the first and second times around at motherhood. Indeed, we will experience in return what we set in motion. However, that is not only in wrong-doing but also in well-doing. We mock and dishonor God when we use His Word, along with our relational titles and spiritual positions in the lives of others, to deceive and bend them to our will. Misappropriating and misquoting scripture to misguide others is spiritual abuse, and spiritual abuse is mocking God.

Doing what we need to do, know to do, and what God has placed in us to do can be hard. Although some may only use this specific scripture like it's a bad thing, we cannot become tired or impatient with doing good, because that, too, shall we reap!

God, I trust what you are doing in my life and in me even when it is unpopular. Remove any anxious cares from me and help me to seek your peace in times of confusion. Make everything concerning your word clear. Amen.

Peace Thirty-Five

"They"

May I never boast except in the cross of our Lord
Jesus Christ, through which the world has been
crucified to me, and I to the world. Neither
circumcision nor uncircumcision means anything;
what counts is the new creation.
Galatians 6:14-15 (NIV)

They said I wanted to leave pretty; they must think I'm superficial and naive. They said that looking at me, no one would ever believe my pain or experiences; they must think I'm lying or exaggerating. They said they thought I had it all together; they must think I'm a fake and failure. Then, they said I didn't love myself because they could never…; they must be better than I am.

Almost nothing can plague us during trials like the "*theys*," for they can be a constant source of judgment and questioning. "They" invade our thoughts daily with what they tell us they think; what we tell ourselves they think; and all their feelings about us they express, or we presume. "***They***" can be exhausting!

That is why we must understand that nothing concerning the deepest, brightest, or darkest matters of our hearts has to evidence "pretty" or otherwise. We do not have to submit to others' assumptions nor perpetuate any narrative they create to pardon that they either don't know us or do know us but neglected to support or attend to us in our life's trenches. The scripture reference is a reminder that, just as Christ was crucified, so was the need to perform any ritual to please Him. Nothing except newness resulting from His crucifixion matters. Paul recognized that he is nothing and can do nothing except by the blood of Jesus. That is what he said he would boast about!

We are affirmed by Christ; therefore, we are not slaves to expectations "they" place on us nor what they say about or think of us and, likewise, "they" do not require our approval. Only what God wills and says matters because *He* is truth and faithfulness.

Christ died on the cross— as did our bondage to sin and servility to the world's opinions and tactics. We have a new life! Jesus has not bound us to rituals and laws to please Him. He has also freed us from performing for the world's approval.

Boast of His sacrifice: everything He has done and continues to do so that we are able to live in the freedom of His forgiveness, peace, and healing! Boast of His grace and mercy that have enabled us to stand

through whatever has passed and is yet to come! Christ is all that matters.

Lord, thank you for the blood that was shed for me! You silence the "theys". Thank you that what used to matter died with you on the cross. Thank you for being a God who feels for me and is faithful to me. Thank you for the peace that comes from being made new in you. Amen.

Peace Thirty-Six

Let God Do His Thing

"...But if you can do anything, take pity on us and help us." "If you can?" said Jesus. "Everything is possible for one who believes." Immediately the boy's father exclaimed, "I do believe; help me overcome my unbelief!" After Jesus had gone indoors, his disciples asked him privately, "Why couldn't we drive it out?" He replied, "This kind can come out only by prayer."
Mark 9:22-24, 28-29 (NIV)

It had been another exhausting day of appointments. I felt very frustrated, and, in my mind, I was repeatedly going over all the ways things still didn't seem to be working for anyone's good. While driving, I silently pleaded with God, for my kids' sakes, to give us new residence and put an end to these long, inconvenient daytrips. They had not asked to live under the guise of a happy family, nor had they asked to struggle to manage under the conditions of adults' poor decisions.

We stopped by a grocery store to pick up some things and take a bathroom break. Her hand clasped tightly in mine, I walked with my daughter, who slowed down and whispered, "You should just calm down and let God do His thing."

Two days later, I was still asking her where she heard those words. To my knowledge, I had never used them and, mostly, I just wondered why she said them to me when and where she had. Her answer remained the same: "I don't know; they just popped in my head."

Oh, the struggle can be so real, but what really is the struggle? I have found that the real struggle, for me, is believing God for a thing when I don't see a thing being done!

Like the father in the scripture, we pray to God because we know what He can do, and we believe He is able; yet we struggle to believe in His will or willingness to answer our prayers. In communicating with Jesus, the man prayed the simplest of prayers: he asked Him for help where he was weak. At times, we all are weak. We become weakened by personal schedules, societal timelines, and social comparisons. Our weakness causes us to measure our problems or needs against God and His power and might. We know He can do what we ask, but our faith starts to entertain questions about whether our concerns are too small for Him to care for or whether they are in excess of what we are worthy and deserving. However, we cannot place God on our clocks or scales. Jesus' helping the man's son and His response to the disciples' question are reminders of His mercy toward us and the importance of confession and prayer, particularly regarding our areas of weakness, and when we are feeling weak as He works.

God, I don't know how or when you're going to work things out, but I know that you can and will. Gift me peace in my racing mind and anxious heart. I confess that I am tired and sometimes doubtful. Help me. Lord, strengthen my faith, and don't forget me. Amen.

Peace Thirty-Seven

Dry Wells

"Are You greater than our father Jacob, who gave us the well, and drank from it himself, as well as his sons and his livestock?" Jesus answered and said to her, "Whoever drinks of this water will thirst again, but whoever drinks of the water that I shall give him will never thirst. But the water that I shall give him will become in him a fountain of water springing up into everlasting life." John 4:12-14 (NKJV)

Nothing compromises the spirit of human relationship quite like having expectations. We expect people in our lives to know their positions and act or respond to us accordingly.

Unfortunately, it is not always that simple. The titles and positions of those we have a relationship with do not always coincide with an individual's willingness to assume certain roles and responsibilities. Much like the woman at the well, we can find ourselves experiencing a thirst that drives us to wells that never satisfy and instead promote an unhealthy, repetitive need or urge to continuously attempt to draw from them out of obligation and/or attachment.

At my most vulnerable, I was always trying to draw from wells that consistently left me thirsty. I remember my therapist saying during one of my sessions, "Tonya, there is no water there." It was at a time when I was most depleted from the constant flow of tears and a persistent thirst for love and the need for others to see and hear me. I learned that many who held positions and titles in my life were dry wells—not empty people—just under-resourced people. They were deficient of what I truly needed and what only God could provide. I had to come to terms with that and learn how to be okay.

The woman asked Jesus, whom she does not know, if He is greater than what had been provided for her by man. Sometimes, those of us who know Jesus and have experienced Him, still forgo expectation in Him as well as relationship and connection with Him for the tangible and immediacy that man offers. The water the woman is speaking of is what she can see, touch, and with which she can quench her thirst immediately—if only for a little while. She must return repeatedly to draw. That is oftentimes the way it is in our relationships: we persist and work ineffectively to retrieve the "water" we need. We compromise, often abandoning His Word, to be temporarily filled by what only Jesus promises to provide and satisfy permanently.

Writing spiritual messages with relatable stories is something I love doing and have done for years. However, I rarely share them because I'm not always certain they will be accepted or understood as I intend. As I am working on this entry, I received what I feel is God's confirmation for the work I am doing right now. A friend texted, "Tonya, draw water from the only wellspring that will never run dry!" I implore you, reader, to do the same!

God, fill me from your well and help me make peace with detachments so that I no longer thirst in dry places. Amen.

Peace Thirty-Eight

Desperate Enough to Wait

Since ancient times no one has heard, no ear has perceived, no eye has seen any God besides you, who acts on behalf of those who wait for him.
Isaiah 64:4 (NIV)

What if people are wrong? What if doing something and making moves are acts of fear, *at times*, and not acts of faith? There were many instances along my journey when individuals, including myself, confused my waiting with fear instead of faith.

It is often advised, especially pertaining to relieving ourselves of unhealthy relationships, that actions for releasing ourselves from them best demonstrate our faith. With the growing abundance of and exposure to self-love and self-care promotions, people who maintain familial and social attachments to persons who treat them poorly or take advantage of them in some way, are perceived as lacking in those areas. They are believed not desperate enough to help themselves because they don't make immediate moves to distance themselves from the relationships or sever their connections.

If only we would consider, in any trial, the amount of desperation it must take to do what appears to be nothing..., or perhaps contemplate how desperate one must be to preserve his or her physical, emotional, and mental well-being to seemingly sit still..., or maybe just take into account the amount of desperation one must feel when his or her only defensive action is inaction, knowing the rewards are not being taken seriously; being seen as stuck or lacking in common sense; and being perceived as void of any positive sense of self..., then, we might judge less, pray more, and solely advise under God's advisement.

Regardless of the trials and/or decisions concerning our relationships, employment, health, or home, we must first seek counsel from the one who goes before us; promises never to leave us, and who will act on our behalf! There is no one like Him!

Many will advise you to do something, make a move, make a choice, take a chance. Know this: you are doing all those things even when you are still and remain steady as you wait. God knows what you need, and patiently awaiting Him with the expectation of His presence, care, and instruction is an act of faith.

It takes a certain degree of strength to look like you're not fighting and still feel like a winner. No one knows what you had to overcome or the obstacles you've just knocked out or kicked down. A certain degree of courage is required to take baby steps when the world only acknowledges those that are giant and leaps. There's a certain degree of determination needed when your lips aren't moving, yet God hears everything you say, as everyone tells you what you should be saying or what they would say. A certain degree of humility is necessary to stand apart and still have love for those who left you because they didn't have patience or understand the desperation of your stillness.

Hold on! You're not alone. Despite how it looks and feels, you are not in this by yourself! It's not about the ones who left, nor is it about those who are with you. It is always, only about *the one and only God*: He who goes before you, who knows what is ahead, and will lead and comfort you through it all. No, your desperation doesn't look like the desperation those who mean well feel or think it should, but it does look as He intended. Your desperation looks like faith and trust in God who orders your steps. Be desperate enough to wait and move how and when He says it's time to move.

God, thank you for help and healing especially in desperate times. You know and see everything. Your knowledge and sight are sufficient and bring peace. It's sometimes hard, especially when I feel misunderstood, but I trust you. I will wait. Amen.

Peace Thirty-Nine

To Protect is to Perfect

*You will keep him in perfect peace, Whose mind is
stayed on You, Because he trusts in You.
Isaiah 26:3 (NKJV)*

It was a sad occasion reuniting with sorority
sisters—many of whom I had not seen in over 25 years.
I remember entering the chapel feeling extremely
anxious inside about that evening of reunion to say
goodbye to one of our own.

Upon seeing one sister in particular, my internal
voice said, "I will have whatever it is she's having."
She was glowing! When we spoke a few days after, I
told her what I whispered to myself when I saw her, and
she said, "It's peace." During our talk, the messages I
kept hearing were about truly surrendering all to God
and praying and trusting that His will be done.

The scripture speaks of perfect peace. Most of what
we hear and see about peace involves protection;
however, little is said about peace perfection which was
clearly what my sorority sister was practicing and
experiencing.

Peaces of Me ♡

Our peace is truly protected when it's perfected, and that perfection comes from a heart surrendered to and mind focused on God. No matter what happens in our lives, when we entrust it all to God, His peace preserves us beyond understanding and typical outcomes.

We often say we are protecting our peace when we decline an invitation or distance ourselves from certain experiences and people. However, the peace of God does not require acts of avoidance, nor is it a retreat or withdrawal from people or problems. Peace is also not a contingency: the problems or issues being experienced do not have to be resolved before peace can be attained. With our minds on God, we can experience peace in the middle of our problems. When we do establish quiet or space to get away from it all, we should be careful not to confuse it with actual peace. Rather, those times are the *conditions* we have created to make connecting with God possible for acquiring the peace we desire. Therefore, it is critical that our hearts and minds are focused on God and trusting Him, because under those conditions, we can either experience Him for our peace, or battle self-defeating thoughts and negative emotions, and remain troubled.

Peace is not a cliché, nor is it to be taken lightly. Saying we desire peace and we're protecting peace means allowing God to make us peaceable in our environments, circumstances, and relationships.

Lord, I want to know your peace. Help me to allow my heart and mind to find perfect, protected peace and rest in you. Amen.

Peace Forty

What Didn't Kill Me Killed the Me...

For you died, and your life is now hidden with Christ in God. Colossians 3:3 (NIV)

Does it really make you stronger, or does what didn't kill you simply allow who you needed to be all along to emerge?

I awakened in the middle of the night, as usual, with fast thoughts of words and phrases flooding my mind. I knew what I had to do. So, I reached for my phone and began typing:

Who was right?
Who was wrong?
Which one of us stayed too long?
Was it him?
Was it me?
Which of us refused to see?
Who couldn't let the other be?
And...
Does fighting hard and long really mean you're strong?

Who fights to feel at home, thinking they truly belong?
Now…
On my own—
I'm a different kind of alone.
I'm learning me—
What it is to be free—
And how to let another be.
God,
What was right?
What was wrong?
Help me never stay…
So broken…
So long…
Again.

My journey to discover the *peaces of me* has not been easy. So much has resurfaced. Things I thought I was over have still been holding me captive. While watching television one day, I observed a young lady being advised by her father to listen with intent and honesty. He told her it was the only way she would know if her friend was lashing out in pain or simply an angry person. I began to consistently ask God to help me do the same, irrespective of persons or their positions, titles, and connections concerning my life.

Today, I am grateful to God for every distressing, intimidating, and painful revelation. I am thankful for the hurt that left me exposed, vulnerable, in pieces, and without peace. I praise God for His love, mercy, and comfort when the hurt was painfully repeated, multiplied, and intensified. I thank God that what didn't kill me killed the me I didn't need to be so I could begin anew, living in the gifts of His presence, love, promises, and purpose!

The scripture's reference to dying and being hidden in Christ is about shedding our former selves to abide and be immersed in His presence and all things acceptable in His sight. What didn't kill me killed the me who was:

- *Anxious and longing for love and family.*
- *Depressed and felt there was nowhere to turn and no one who would believe or understand her.*
- *Begging to be heard and understood.*
- *Shrinking and conforming so others were more comfortable than she.*
- *An over-thinker trying to read faces, catch cues, and comprehend silence.*
- *A people-pleaser who neglected herself.*

At some point we all find ourselves in pieces searching for our *peaces* only to be found in the safety of Jesus. Many times, it was difficult to process and understand that God wasn't simply allowing me to be wounded, but He was wounded for me, so that the wounds I would suffer could heal me. All the hurt and disappointments were guiding me to *Him*. Every day brings new perspectives and, sometimes, there is an old or new piece to process and make peace. Still, I trust that what God has let live is safe, and I praise Him for creating the difference.

Dear God, thank you for my journey. Thank you for every broken piece that has revealed and created Peaces of Me. Amen.

*To God be the glory for His
faithfulness and inability to fail!*

Personal Reflections

They must turn from evil and do good; they must seek peace and pursue it. 1 Peter 3:11 (NIV)

- Peace with God: learning to accept and receive God's gifts and will for my life and relationships.

- Peace with Others: understanding that God's gifts of salvation, forgiveness, and compassion are for all of us—even those I feel have offended or hurt me.

- Peace Within: resisting urges to engage in verbal and/or physical acts of malevolence; moving past the hurt and offense to follow peacefulness; living by faith; and walking in forgiveness.

Having peace in every area of our lives requires focus, and that focus entails being on one accord with God. When we prioritize and rely on a reconciled, harmonious relationship with God, we can live a life of peace with Him that affords us peace within ourselves for living in peace with His people, so that He may be glorified!

In loving memory of

Richard Depugh

Henry Lee McNeil

Sally Dell McNeil

and

James Herbert Underwood

Notes

Akers, D. (1953). Lead Me, Guide Me. [Song recorded by Dorothy Simmons, Doris Akers]. *New National Baptist Hymnal.*
Hymnology Archivehttps://www.hymnologyarchive.c om › ...Lead Me, Guide Me

Allender, D.B. (2005). *To be told: God invites you to coauthor your future*. WaterBrook.

Entwistle, D. N. (2015). *Integrative approaches to psychology and Christianity: An introduction to worldview issues, philosophical foundations, and models of integration.* Cascade Books, An Imprint of Wipf and Stock Publishers.

Eugene, A.C., Jr. [@thisisalbaner]. (2022, September 30). The voices pt.1. [Video File] Retrieved from Instagram.
https://Instagram.com/thisisalbaner?igshid=NTc4MTl wNjQ2YQ==

Hawkins, Dr. R. & Clinton, Dr. T. (2015). *The new Christian counselor: A fresh biblical & transformational* approach. Harvest House Publishers.

Hui, E., Broom, B., & Guthrie, N. (Hosts). (2023, January 25). Suffering, sorrow, and grief (S2 No. 63) [Audio podcast episode] In Counsel for Life. https://podcasts.apple.com/us/podcast/suffering-sorrow-and-grief-featuring-nancy-guthrie/id1581983614?i=1000596479194

Isabella, T., Von Eeden, T., & Akil, S. (Writers) & Boom, B. (Producer). (2018, February 27). Three Sevens: The Book of Thunder (Season 1, Episode 6) [TV series episode]. S. Akil, M.B. Akil, G. Berlanti, & S. Schechter (Executive Producers). *Black Lightning*. Berlanti Productions; Akil Productions; DC Entertainment; & Warner Bros. Television.

Jakes, T.D. [T.D Jakes Ministries]. (2021, August 12). Defense against offenses: Get out of your feelings. [Video]. YouTube. https://you.tu.be/6J2pc68KMUw

Shirer, P. [The Chat with Priscilla]. (2018, August 8). Hope heals (part one). [Video]. YouTube. https://youtu.be/M-Z76LC23L4?si=doBqosa696hBB-RD

@taurenwells. (2022, July 22). Tauren Wells: joy in the morning. [Video File]. Retrieved from Instagram. https://Instagram.com/taurenwells?igshid=NTc4MTlwNjQ2YQ==

Made in the USA
Columbia, SC
06 November 2024

45838542R00088